STEPH "THE HAMMER" HAMMERMAN

DRIVEN

HOW ADVERSITY HELPED ME
FIND MY GREATEST POTENTIAL

For more information, to inquire about rights to this or other works, or to purchase copies for special educational, business, or sales promotional uses, please write to:

Incorgnito Publishing Press
1651 Devonshire Lane
Sarasota, FL 34236
888-859-0792
Contact@incorgnitobooks.com

FIRST EDITION

Printed in the United States of America

ISBN: 978-1944589806

10 9 8 7 6 5 4 3 2 1

DEDICATION

For Grandma and Grandpa. You afforded me every opportunity to experience a life that would have been impossible without your love and support. Thank you for believing in my dreams even before I knew what they were. I love you!

Life's like one big conga line. You can either choose to sit it out and miss the fun or hop on in and join the party. I choose to party!

CONTENTS

FOREWORD

When Steph presented me with the opportunity to compose the foreword to *Driven*, I suddenly found myself inundated with apprehension and doubt. The quintessential foreword is penned by vetted subject matter experts, persons of academic pedigree, or individuals of notable celebrity—all attributes that elude my constitution. The following days, I spent reminiscing over the past six years with the now Mrs. Roach, pondering what I could possibly contribute to aid the reader in understanding the incredible woman who captured my heart and renewed my sense of empathy. Then it hit me.

When we met, Steph worked very long hours, six or seven days a week. This left little time for the obligatory trips to the store and even less for dates. We always chose to make the most of the situation by going shopping or running errands together.

One late night, an unusually tired Steph and I made the trip to a desolate grocery store. The employees were collecting carts in the empty parking lot, and it became obvious to us that we were the only shoppers. We hastened through the aisles, retrieving our items in an effort to get her home, rested, and ready for the 4:00 a.m. start to her day.

While waiting in the checkout line, a child of about eight years old approached Steph from behind and touched her leg. Steph was so startled, she nearly jumped out of her chair! The little boy, who was on the autism spectrum, had wandered away from his father, who was a couple of registers away from us.

Steph quickly composed herself and said, "Hello, what's your name?" The boy pointed at Steph's leg and said, "I hope you feel better." The boy's father, embarrassed and scared, came running over trying to apologize, but Steph just continued her conversation with the boy.

"Aw, thank you! Have you ever seen a wheelchair before? It's pretty cool, right? Can you tell me how many wheels it has?"

At that moment, I happened to glance at the boy's father. Observing his son's innocent expression of empathy being reciprocated with kind words and acceptance had literally brought him to tears...quickly followed by my own. Steph told the father he was doing a great job and that it was a pleasure to meet him and his son. On the ride home, we discussed just how badly that interaction could have gone for the wrong recipient, and judging by the father's reaction, it probably had in the past.

Why do I tell you this story? Simply put, it was in that brief moment of compassion, witnessing Steph's genuine expression of empathy for a stranger, that I knew I'd fallen in love with her. The ironic part of this story is that only a few weeks later, Steph would be diagnosed with cancer. Maybe the little man was on to something.

While *Driven* chronicles the adventures, struggles,

and triumphs of Steph's path-paving journey, it's only a small glimpse into the true character of the amazing woman I'm so blessed to be going through life with. I hope that her model of hard work and perseverance is one you'll adopt in your own endeavors, but I'd also encourage you to take notice of the underlying subtleties of empathy. The real impact of "The Hammer" isn't in the big moments of life; it's in the little ones, the ones that often mean the most!

—Tyler Roach

INTRODUCTION

Oh, to have been a fly on that wall thirty-two years ago when my parents were told they were having twins. I can't imagine how they must have been feeling. But with my twin brother and I born only nine and a half months after our older brother, I have no doubt they were terrified.

Two small babies, born at thirty weeks, one weighing only one pound and fifteen ounces and the other not much bigger at three pounds and five ounces, were brought into this world before they were ready to live outside the safety of their mother's warm womb. I have seen the home video of my brother and me just after we were released from the hospital. How tiny we were. I was still connected to a heart monitor and, in the video, you can hear the thing sound off at least twenty times. Watching that video put me in my family's shoes in a real way. When I watch it, every time that alarm sounds, I become the worried parent behind the camera, fearful that something is wrong with my precious baby. It couldn't have been easy for my parents or extended family to have lived those moments, trying to monitor two preemies while having to care for a one-year-old at the same time.

I was the smaller of the two. I've been told I put up a

good fight because when my brother came out, he was black and blue. I came out first, four minutes before him to be exact. It was made clear early on that our lives would be vastly different. A few short weeks after I was born, I was diagnosed with Cerebral Palsy (CP), a group of disorders that affect a person›s ability to move and maintain balance and posture. According to the CDC, CP is the most common motor disability in childhood. Cerebral means having to do with the brain. Palsy means weakness or problems with using the muscles. CP is definitely not a one-size-fits-all affliction. Each person is affected differently, so my future was unclear. The doctors didn't know exactly what kind of quality of life I would have, but they would prepare my entire family for the real possibility that I would never read, speak, write, or walk.

If only those same doctors could see me now. It's hard not to smile while writing this story. Thirty-two years ago, people were making plans for the real eventuality that I would never make it out of the hospital alive. But the universe and I had other plans.

As mentioned earlier, CP manifests differently in every person who experiences it. For me, it affects both my upper and lower body. My right side is weaker than my left, and I need some sort of assistive device (i.e. a walker, crutches, or a wheelchair) to be able to get around independently. I'm like a real-life Barbie who comes with great hair and a plethora of accessories to choose from.

All jokes aside, I won't sugarcoat anything or say that life was or is ever easy, but I think my life's blueprint has worked out exactly as it was meant to be, and although I have to do things a bit differently than the average person, I have learned that being born a little different has opened up my life to opportunities I never imagined were possible.

This story is mine. About how I learned to take my life's adversities and turn them into a blazing fire of triumph. This book is *for* you. While my stories and experiences paint a picture of *my* life, it is my hope that embarking on this journey together enables *you* to dig down deep, reflect on *your* life experiences, and realize that *you* are capable of way more than *you* might give *yourself* credit for.

THE FOUNDATION

My life started out pretty "normal" (other than the whole CP thing). I was fortunate to be born into a family where I wanted for nothing. A mom, a dad, an older brother, a twin, all living in a beautiful house on Long Island, New York. It wouldn't be long before our little sister was added to our family just three years later. We all developed vastly different personalities and, over the last almost three decades, have been through a lot together as well as individually.

My older brother is and has always been intellectually gifted. He always got straight A's, is fluent in multiple languages, and attended an Ivy League college. Truthfully, it wasn't always easy finding common ground. He knows *a lot* about a lot and doesn't like to be wrong. Playing Jeopardy with him is quite annoying because he often knows most of the answers even before the entire question is read! In all seriousness, though, my big brother has continually found ways to create his own success, and that's something I truly admire. He is very independent, and oftentimes, I wish I was able to express myself to others as directly as he does.

My womb mate and I probably have the most things in common, though I'm not sure we have the whole twin

ESP thing that some sets of twins experience. From our taste in music to the people we chose to call friends throughout our grade school years, we were very similar. He may not know this, but my twin brother has always been someone who helped drive me to want to be as independent as possible.

As we developed into our own unique individuals though, our personalities became quite the opposite. By the age of three, I had become loud and talkative while my brother was reserved and kept to himself. To this day, he is able to let things just roll off his back and go with the flow, whereas I need to feel all of my experiences very deeply. Nowadays, when we tell people we are twins, they often laugh because we don't even remotely look alike, and our height difference is staggering. I stand at a solid four feet, eleven inches on a good day, while he towers over me at six-foot-one.

Having a baby sister to play with when I was three was like having a life-sized baby doll. I might not have been able to help dress her up in different outfits, but I could hold her and help her learn how to crawl. I had mastered that movement by the time I was three.

My sister and I grew up very close. Her bedroom connected to mine, and we often played games together and used our imaginations to create intricate stories. One of my favorite games we'd play was called typewriter. We would get under our bed covers and pretend to type letters to each other as if we couldn't hear one another. It would make us giggle and laugh for hours. My sister had a large imagination. She even created a character named Rupert who would do the craziest, silliest, and sometimes really bad things, like drawing on the walls of her bedroom. When our parents realized all the havoc "he" was causing, they explained to us that Rupert would not be returning because they had "sent him on a rocket ship to live on the moon." We still laugh about that today. My sister is strong-willed, hardworking, and for most of my life, the one who would physically help me with a lot of things when others didn't want to. She grew up a lot faster than most her age, and it sometimes felt like she took on the role of my "big" little sister.

My parents were married for nineteen years, and from what I saw through the lens of a child's innocence, they seemed to be having a pretty wonderful life. We were part of a rather large extended family, almost all of us living on Long Island. We had a great support system with both sets of grandparents and five pairs of aunts and uncles. Our mom has one sister, and our father is one of four children. Our maternal grandparents were affectionately known as "Nana" and "Poppy," and our paternal grandparents were lovingly known as Grandpa and Grandma.

There was a lot of love to go around, but I have always had a unique bond with Grandpa. From the moment I was born, Grandpa and Grandma have been my biggest fans, greatest support system, and have afforded me every opportunity to live the happiest and healthiest possible life.

There is a photograph of Grandpa smiling ear to ear while visiting my brother and me as we lay in an incubator in the hospital NICU hours after we had arrived that I adore. Apparently, he pretended to be a doctor to get access to see us after visiting hours were over. He didn't fool anyone, especially the nurse who took the photo. She told him he could spend a few moments with us. She is the one who snapped the photo, and then she kicked him out of the NICU. I don't have a recollection of that actual moment in time, but man, am I glad he still has that Polaroid. They say a picture is worth a thousand words. That may be true for some, but to me, that picture is priceless.

As I began to grow, so did the list of doctor appointments. Living with cerebral palsy meant that I needed a lot more medical care at first, from physical therapists to occupational therapists, neurologists to surgeons. Most of these appointments would happen in New York City, and Grandpa would make the best effort he could to be there along with my parents as they navigated this new life raising a child with a physical disability. I appreciate it now more than ever because I now understand that at the time, Grandpa was a high-level executive at Merrill Lynch, and his job came with great responsibilities. He worked many long days, but he always made it a point to be invested in my life and, quite honestly, all of his grandchildren's lives. With thirteen grandchildren at the time, that was no easy task, but both of my grandparents made their love and support for each of us seem effortless.

From what I can remember from my early childhood, my parents were both very supportive, loving, and wanting to make sure they did everything they could to keep me involved in activities just like my siblings. While my brothers played Little League, I rode horses at a program dedicated to working with the adaptive population. While my sister took gymnastics, I took swimming lessons, which were where I learned to feel the most freedom.

Our weekends were filled with play dates, extracurricular activities, and sleepovers with our cousins. All of the cousins were very close in age, so during the earlier years of our lives, it felt like we were growing up with a whole army of brothers and sisters!

Growing up in this type of family, when my extended family members were cognizant of my differences but never made them a big deal, shaped me into the person I am. If I wanted to do something, I had to find a way to get it done even if that meant taking three times as long as everyone else. If anyone told me they thought I couldn't or shouldn't do something, I had all the more burning desire to prove them wrong, and I did everything in my power to do just that.

THE POWER OF CHOICE

"I seek opportunity, not security. I will not trade my dignity for a handout. It is my heritage to think and act for myself." — Dr. Henry Viscardi

I had no idea how impactful this man and his school would become in my young life. Dr. Viscardi founded the Viscardi School in 1962, in Albertson, New York. The first of its kind, the Henry Viscardi School was a place where children with physical disabilities and rare illnesses could attend school and have access to a variety of resources such as medical care and, if needed, physical, occupational, and speech therapy. The school caters to students up to the age of twenty-one. I attended the Viscardi School for Pre-K and Kindergarten.

One of the most common questions I get asked is, "Where do you find your motivation?" My answer is, "I have two big motivators: Brandon and Scott." Those two boys were my closest friends at Viscardi. They happened to be the most attractive boys in the class. At three years old, I was a big flirt. After spending a short time at school, I told my parents that I had a husband. His name was Brandon. We skipped the dating part; I just loved him, so he had to be my husband. To a three-year-old, that made perfect sense. To my parents, not so much. But when I think back as an adult on the love I felt for Brandon, it still seems sensible to me. I loved the way he looked at me and smiled at me, and I can remember what it felt like to hold his tightly clenched hand.

Like me, Brandon was a twin and, like me Brandon had CP. But, unlike me, he couldn't walk at all. In fact, he didn't walk, talk, or write, but to me, he was perfect. We had our own language. He would talk with his eyes that lit up every time we were together. We had a unique connection that was obvious to everyone around us at the time, from our parents to his nurses, to our teachers. I don't have many memories of that age, but the memories I have of Brandon and I are so clear, it feels like if I were to close my eyes, I could be transported back to those moments in time. I loved every second of growing up with Brandon.

Socializing was a big part of my life even at a young age. I loved going to play dates with friends and using our imaginations to entertain ourselves, but something about going to Brandon's house was special. Brandon loved food, and he loved cooking. While he couldn't physically cook the meals himself, he would use his eyes to communicate what ingredients needed to go where, and someone would do the physical work for him or sometimes with him. I remember that one time, his dad, Alan, took us to the grocery store. As Brandon picked out the ingredients, his eyes would light up. He might not have known how all the ingredients fit together, but it was as if he *knew* whatever we were going to make was going to taste delicious (gourmet food in the eyes of a three- to five-year-old).

I loved how supportive his parents were. They knew Brandon's life was going to come with plenty of challenges, but they did everything in their power to treat him with respect and allow him to experience as much normalcy as possible. These play dates were filled with many laughs, a lot of love, and innocence.

The harsh reality of cerebral palsy, as I mentioned, is that it comes in all different forms and can affect each individual who lives with it differently. While I was able to move around relatively independently and communicate freely, Brandon required around-the-clock care and assistive devices to communicate. As we grew older, I was able to experience the world and all it had to offer while Brandon's body began to work against him.

As the years went by, and Brandon and I were separated by distance and life changes, our contact with one another grew infrequent. Brandon spoke one audible word to me his entire life: "car." After many years of therapy, he had learned how to say "car," and during a conversation over the phone, he was able to share that moment with me. I was probably nine or ten when I got that call. He was so proud, and I was so proud of him. Brandon was one of the most intelligent, kind-hearted, and genuine people I have ever known. He didn't need an extensive vocabulary to show you how much he cared. Our friendship was unspoken but always understood; words could not have made our affection or our understanding any clearer.

Just before my twenty-seventh birthday, I learned that Brandon had passed away. When I heard of his passing,

I was shaken to my core. I know deep down that he's at peace now. I like to think he has found his forever love and is professing it from the rooftops. It's ironic that when people we love pass on, it reminds us to keep on living, but that's exactly what Brandon has done for me. He will forever be the first person I gave my heart to, and I am better because of him.

The Viscardi School helped to lay the foundation for my level of independence and social skills. I formed some great friendships there, and the school helped me to build a strong foundation for my educational and social development. Their early work with me, strengthening my vocal and coordination skills, was invaluable. Still, other than forging two very impactful friendships there, I never truly felt like I belonged. Knowing that a place like this still exists is nothing short of amazing.

***

At the end of my kindergarten year, I was given a choice that changed the course of my life. My parents sat me down and asked me a simple question: "Do you want to go to school with your brothers?" I did. I knew I wanted to be doing the same things as my siblings, so I chose a new school where I would not only make new friends and meet new challenges but would learn a lot more about my family's culture. My siblings and I attended Brandeis, a Jewish school.

From day one, this new school felt right. I began making new friends, got to see my siblings during the day, and began learning a second language, Hebrew, for the first time. I may have moved differently than everyone else, but to me, being around bi-peds (people who walk on two feet-chair user joke) all day, made me feel "normal." It's a hard thing to admit, but I knew that once I started attending this school, I wouldn't want to go back to an environment where everyone looked like me.

At six years old, I learned the meaning of a few commonly used terms when referencing a child who has any sort of need for special accommodations. For example, I learned I would be making the transition to a "mainstream setting," meaning that everyone around me was able-bodied and the majority of the students wouldn't need any sort of special accommodations. I would be given an IEP (a document that outlines the accommodations needed) that would evolve along with me until I graduated from high school.

I took the bus to school every day, and I loved it. I walked the halls with my walker and would later get more confident in using my crutches. I had an aide who made sure I got to class safely and could keep up with things like note-taking and test-taking. My first aide was Gloria, and she was wonderful. She was a friend and a guide and knew just when to insert herself as my helper and when to let me figure life out on my own. She helped me get through the day without incident but stayed in the background when I needed to be "me" with friends and at recess. Her influence has stuck with me through the years.

Learning how to walk with crutches, putting in my contact lenses, and even learning how to brush my hair took a lot of physical and occupational therapy. From the age of about three to the age of fifteen, I would regularly be pulled out of classes to attend one or another therapy. It became a nuisance and attracted unwanted attention as I progressed in school grades, but looking back now, I'm so grateful to have had access to all of those resources.

I learned to do all the things the doctors once told my parents to be prepared for me not to do. I was able to clearly speak and communicate my thoughts and feelings. I was able to read and, although it took (and still takes) a little bit longer than the average person, I learned to write. That therapy laid the foundation for what I am able to do now and for how much more I intend to do. To this day, I remain close with my two physical therapists and often remind them of the impact they had on my earlier years.

Attending the same school as my siblings gave me a lot of confidence. I was very social and loved to be involved with friends and the other kids in my classes. From birthday parties to weekend play dates and other activities, I was always staying busy, and despite my parents' worries, all the kids at the new school accepted me. People sometimes ask me if I've ever experienced bullying, and there's only one incident that I remember, which is ironic because it involves a concussion. His name was Josh. He was a school bully, and he showed me the same lack of courtesy as he would the able-bodied kids. One day, for no apparent reason (do bullies ever reason?), he pulled my crutches swiftly out from under me while I was walking ahead of my aide in the school hallway. I hit my head so hard, I ended up with a concussion. I think he might have been more scared by the incident than I was because, after that, he never bothered me again. It's odd that someone as insignificant as he should stand out in my memory of a time that was so full of wonderful experiences. Maybe I remember him because he was an outlier. I truly do hope he's changed his ways and is doing great things with his life now.

Josh aside, one of the fondest memories I have of how supportive the people at my new school were was when my first-grade teacher, Mrs. Dreyfus, surprised me by making a class field trip experience out of my very first adaptive athletic event, the Empire State Games. The event spanned two days and was intended for physically challenged athletes to compete in various Olympic-style events; the top three in each event even got to go home with medals. I competed in three sports at the games: track, swimming, and equestrian. I have no idea why I chose those three, but when race day arrived, I was excited to show off my skills. I remember seeing my parents, teacher, and all of my classmates in these bright yellow hats that read, "GO STEPHIE GO" along with a big sign they made to support me. It was a pretty awesome feeling. In these races, we didn't go a long distance, and I had someone next to me to make sure I didn't fall, but when I crossed the finish line of that first race and saw all of my friends there to support me, I felt like I had just run the biggest race of my life. For many of my classmates, it was the first time being around kids our age and older who had different abilities. I like to think it was a one-of-a-kind field trip that they never forgot.

I took home an assortment of medals that weekend, all different colors. The heavy medals hung proudly around my neck, and I smiled widely when I realized what I had accomplished. And as I smiled, my athletic aspirations began to take root and grow deep within my soul. That dream would continue to blossom and eventually mature into a much greater life purpose.

It was around that same time that I started to develop a passion for writing and, through some disability resource connections, I was introduced to the people at *WE* magazine. Now out of circulation, it was a magazine dedicated to celebrating the lives and accomplishments of people living with various disabilities as well as resources available to better the lives of the greater disability community.

At seven years old, I was given my first writing assignment. I had been granted the prestigious title of "toy editor" for the magazine, and I took this job very seriously. Once a month, I would be sent a box of some of the newest toys on the market, and I would be asked to write a review of the toy and how accessible it was for people in the community. It was probably one of the most fun jobs I've ever had, and it also led to one of the best opportunities I've ever been given. I was seven when I appeared on CNN for the first time to deliver a live review of Mattel's newest Barbie friend, Wheelchair Becky.

I was no stranger to having cameras in my face or being interviewed even at a young age (more on that later), but the most ironic thing about this interview was that I had never actually seen the doll before the interview. Right before the news anchor started asking me questions, I caught a glimpse of a picture of the doll in the corner of my eye, and when they asked me a question about the doll, I responded strictly based on my reaction to the picture. My mom tells people that that was the moment everyone knew I would be just fine and able to advocate for myself as needed. Whatever came out of my mouth that evening made me look like I was well-prepared for the interview and truly enjoyed playing with Becky. In the end, it was a win-win: The interview was a hit, and I got to take home the groundbreaking new doll.

As I continued to navigate what it meant to live with cerebral palsy while growing up in a mostly able-bodied world, my parents tried to expose me to opportunities that would allow me to feel like a "normal" kid, all while showing the world that living with different abilities doesn't necessarily have one definition. Along with physical therapy and occupational therapy sessions, and spending time with my friends and my siblings, my mom got me into child modeling. I'm not certain how this came about. Maybe someone from a toy company saw me with my mom and they needed diverse kids in their ads. Maybe it was an agent who was friends with a family we knew. However it happened, I soon had an agent getting me bookings. At the age of six, I began getting booked for photo shoots and commercials with some of the biggest companies at the time: Toys R Us, Kids R Us, *Good Housekeeping*, Tower Records, and even FAO Schwartz.

It was a fun time in my young life. I loved dressing up, I loved meeting new people, and it became obvious during my first photo shoot that I was the furthest thing from being camera shy.

I felt like I had the coolest "job." The staff at the commercial shoots did my hair and makeup, dressed me up in the latest kid fashions, and made me feel like a princess. There was a lot of standing during these shoots, so my mom came up with a key phrase, *tall-standing,* a cue to remind me to stand tall and maintain good posture while they were shooting. There were days when I would have to leave school early to get to a shoot, and I can remember being picked up in a black town car and heading into New York City. Every time I got into the car, I knew I was going to have the opportunity to do something fun. My grandpa was a busy man, but because he worked in the city, he would often take time out of his day and meet us at the different shoot locations. He was so supportive. Sometimes, he would take me out to lunch afterward and make it our day together. When I think back to a lot of these experiences from my early years, it amazes me that I was granted such exceptional opportunities. Not many kids can say they were a model or got to be on national television talking about a history-making doll, but I did, and those are moments I will always be grateful for.

Like all good times, my time as a model had to eventually come to an end. For me, it was during a Kids R Us children's coat drive photo shoot. The shoot was for the December cover, but we filmed it in July. Covers and the related content inside magazines take a long time to put together, so you have to start months in advance. To make the cover look authentic, we were dressed in complete winter paraphernalia: winter coat, thick socks, mittens, and a hat. We had to stand there for hours dressed like that in the middle of July. That took the glory out of modeling for this little princess and put an end to my modeling days—it was no longer fun!

Representation of people living with different abilities has come a long way since my first appearance on CNN, but knowing that I was able to use my voice and create a positive narrative at a young age was powerful. Looking back on those experiences, I'm glad I was able to help set an example for other little girls like me in the future.

While I was doing all of these amazing things in front of the camera, I still wanted to be just like everyone else. One thing that was very common for kids to do in the summer, especially for Jewish upper-middle-class families, was to go to sleep-away camp. At seven years old, I came home from school and told my mom that one of my best friends, Jessica, was going to camp for the summer and that I was going to go with her. My parents had never told us that sleep-away camp was an option before, but if many of my friends were going, why couldn't I? It was simple seven-year-old logic, right?

I'm certain there were numerous steps in between, but after a conversation with Jessica's parents and learning more about the camp, my parents decided to contact the directors to see if it would be a possibility, and they'd take it from there. Located in the Catskill Mountains in upstate New York, about three hours from our house, was Camp Chipinaw. It was close enough in case of an emergency but felt far enough away that missing home wasn't out of the question. We went to visit the camp during the fall season. It was chilly, the trees were losing their leaves, and we had to bundle up a bit, but to a seven-year-old girl, this place looked to be as much fun as Disney World.

There were small wooden buildings lined up all along the lake. They had a uniform look: red and green roofs and porches painted white. Each building looked exactly the same; the only way to tell them apart was by the numbers and letters painted on the front doors.

I learned that those were called bunkhouses, and they were where the campers and counselors slept. As we continued the tour, we learned all about the rich history of the camp. It was actually built as a summer camp for boys in 1926. Twelve years later, the girls' campus was added. The dining hall was filled with camp history. Painted plaques, each one representing a bunkhouse from the past to the present, were hung on the walls. There were traditional songs and chants, talent shows, and color war games, all depicted on one wall or another, all little pieces of history. From one look, I just knew this was something I had to be a part of. Even as a seven-year-old girl, I knew by fitting in here and succeeding at this camp, I would be given the opportunity to help show others like me that a summer away from home was possible.

We had the opportunity to meet the owners, Stan and Joan Rubin. They were such kind and welcoming people.

They were probably in their early sixties at the time, and I could just tell they were full of love and passion for this place. They reminded me a lot of my own grandparents, and from the first meeting, they made me feel safe and seen. They were very open-minded to the idea of me coming to camp, even sharing with me that they had a granddaughter my age who would be starting as a camper the same summer.

I left our tour feeling hopeful, but there were still a few details that needed to be ironed out. I used hot-pink crutches to get around, but I also used a stroller at the time for navigating long distances. I still needed help to safely get dressed, shower, and get from place to place, so it was made clear to me that I would be assigned a one-on-one counselor if I were to go to camp. I was so excited! After a few months of waiting and phone calls back and forth with the camp, I learned that I was going!

It would be two whole months away from home, experiencing the camp with Jessica and hopefully making many more friends. I couldn't believe it. About a month before heading to the camp, we had to pack my bag. The camp sends you a suggested list; you pack the duffel bag, someone picks it up, and all of your stuff is there waiting for you when you get there. It seemed like magic, but knowing now how much work my mom put into labeling all my clothes, packing my necessities, and making sure everything got there safely, it's pretty incredible. I remember telling anyone who would listen that I was going to sleep-away camp. It felt like I had been given a chance to prove to people what I was capable of doing, and I wasn't going to waste the opportunity.

The morning of the beginning of my summer adventure finally came. I anxiously climbed aboard the bus and waved goodbye to my parents as the bus pulled away. I can't exactly remember the feeling going through my little body, but I remember feeling excited and proud for trying something new. Jessica and I sat next to each other, taking the front seat. I remember feeling like I was on one of the rollercoaster rides at Disney World when we would go up the huge hills, reach the peak, and roll downhill. I'm pretty sure it helped the three-hour drive go by faster.

When our bus finally pulled into CHIPINAW with all the other buses, there were probably close to fifty staff members, wearing red polo shirts with CHIPINAW in white letters, to greet us. They were clapping, whistling, smiling, and waving their arms in the air; you could feel the excitement. When the doors opened, Jessica and I let everyone else out first. It was going to take a bit longer for me to maneuver myself to the door of the bus, and she understood that better than anyone. Once empty, Jess climbed over me, gathered our things, and waited for me to come down. At the bottom of the stairs, I was greeted by a young counselor named Brad. He had dark curly hair covered by a blue baseball cap and the biggest smile. Brad extended his arms and gave me a huge hug, lifting me off the ground and then helping me safely touch the ground. Just like that, I felt accepted and welcome with open arms (literally); it was the best feeling ever.

The directors and staff made an effort to make me feel

welcome and included. They even built a ramp on the side of my bunk to make sure it was accessible for me whether I was walking or rolling. I remembered Stan telling me he had a granddaughter my age who would be starting camp, and to my surprise, she was in my cabin. Her name was Alexa. She was quiet and shy, but she was so pretty and was one of the first people there to ask to be my friend. It was as though Stan knew that we needed each other; we became the closest of friends that summer.

Summer at camp moves quickly. One minute you're saying hello and getting to know your cabin mates and sending your first letter home, and the next thing you know, you're knee-deep in arts and crafts, singing songs, going to activities, and then it's halfway through the summer and you're getting ready for visiting day. Visiting day was the one day when your parents and other family members could come visit you, bring you candy, attend a barbecue, do activities with you, and watch the various shows put on by campers. My parents, siblings, and grandparents all came to visiting day. I had written them a few letters telling them I had a surprise for when they came to visit, but I wouldn't tell them what it was.

The camp had offered us the opportunity to go to "circus" as an elective activity. It was there where we could learn how to do circus acts like roller skating, juggling, and a few magic tricks. But the biggest attraction was learning how to perform on the trapeze. Campers could learn how to fly, tumble, and do all sorts of complicated routines. Given my innate desire toward doing things I shouldn't or supposedly couldn't do, I was determined to do everything I could to fly on that trapeze. Despite all the odds stacked against me, I still needed to try.

The trapeze was twenty-five feet in the air. *How was I going to get up there?* All the other campers could climb the rungs of the ladder that dangled off the side of the platform, but that clearly was not going to be an option for me. When I made it known that this was something I wanted to surprise my family with on visiting day, the circus specialists and the counselors partnered to find a way to make it happen. They figured out how to clip a pulley to a harness that would wrap around me and then be used to pull me up. At first, I was really scared. but knowing that the circus folks were experts in this field made me feel safe. They wanted to help me have the same experience as any other camper, and their ded-ication to that goal made me enjoy the experience even more.

I practiced for about two weeks before my family's ar-rival. My fellow circus-goers were learning how to fly, catch, and hang upside down from the bar; it looked like a lot of fun, but I knew my reality was going to look a lit-tle different. My tiny hands would just have to hold onto the bar as tight as I could and let my body just pendulum swing.

When the moment arrived and my family and every-one else were finally going to see me on the trapeze, I was anxious. All of the what-ifs and doubt started to en-ter my mind. Bruce was the leading circus specialist. He was tall and muscular but had a very calming energy.

He took my hands, looked me in the eye, smiled at me, and told me he would never let anything bad happen to me. I believed him. I remember being clipped into the harness and being slowly hoisted up. We had done this so many times, but this time it was real. I was going to do something many didn't want to dare to try. Maybe it wasn't going to look as pretty as doing tricks in the air some others were doing, but I had CP, and I *was* going to be up there swinging on that trapeze.

As the ground got farther away from me and the platform got closer, I looked up and saw another specialist smiling at me, reminding me what I had to do with my hands. As I reached the top, they grabbed me, held me tight, and helped me get steady on my feet. This probably took a lot longer and was not necessarily part of the full show, but every single staff member who was there that day was invested in wanting to see me successfully fly on that trapeze. Once I was steady, they chalked up my hands and told me to grab the bar tight. I could hear my family screaming down below, and others were clapping. Once I had a good grip on the bar, the countdown began: "Three, two, one ... have fun!" My feet left the platform, my legs went stiff as a board, and I was flying! It was exhilarating. I swung back and forth four or five times and then landed in the net below me. I don't think anyone thought that I would actually attempt something so daring, but at the end of it all, I was met with hugs, high-fives, and a lot of support.

After my heroics at the circus ended, I brought my family back to my bunk and introduced them to friends and counselors, and showed off a few of the masterpieces I had created during arts and crafts. The day had gone as fast as it had arrived. By the end, my parents not only signed me up for another summer, but they fielded inquiries from my siblings about joining me as well.

My first summer at Chipinaw was such an incredible experience that it led to returning for five more summers. The zip code 12783 became part of the address of my second home, a place where friends became family and memories were made that stood the test of time. My time at that camp left an imprint on my soul and at the same time made me feel proud knowing that my presence there helped educate others and allowed people to see what is possible when you give yourself permission to try.

As time went on, life got a little more challenging, and after five summers, I had to say goodbye to a place that had become such a big part of me. My summers away from home taught me a great deal about advocacy and resilience, and what we are truly capable of if we want something bad enough. I was going to need all of these skills more than ever as I began to navigate through some of the toughest moments that would inevitably shape me into the woman I am today.

LIFE LESSONS AND
GUARDIAN ANGELS

In 2005, when I was fifteen and several years removed from my Chipinaw experiences, my parents had
me attend another summer camp: Southampton Fresh
Air Home (SFAH) in Southampton, New York. This
one was for kids with physical disabilities. I had gone
through major reconstructive surgery a few years prior
and wasn't moving around the same way I used to, and
I think my parents thought I would be safer there than
with my usual camp crowd.

It's quite embarrassing to admit now, but I *hated* the
thought of this. Being around so many people with different disabilities truthfully made me feel uncomfortable.
It was like someone was trying to put me in a box. I just
never truly felt like I identified with this community. It's
not that I thought I was better than anyone or above being part of this community; I had just grown up in such
an able-bodied world that it was hard for me to see that
it was okay to be accepted and part of both communities.

I'm ashamed to admit that it has taken me an extremely long time to truly allow myself to identify with others
with disabilities, especially CP, but the summer at SFAH
gave me the opportunity to crack open the door and open

my heart and mind to experiences and people I wouldn't otherwise have in my life.

Scott Pollock Jr. was one of those people. People called him Scotty, and his loved ones called him "Bubba." Scotty had a smile that lit up a room. He was filled with so much swagger that when he entered a room, everyone wanted to grab his attention. We were classmates at Viscardi when we were three years old. Scotty was one of the most unique and talented individuals I have ever met. You see, he was born with no arms, and his legs were two different lengths, so for as long as I can remember, Scotty got around with a custom-built power chair with the controls placed down by one of his legs. I don't think I ever noticed that he was different than most kids. To me, he was always just Scotty. As we got older, Scott decided to stay at Viscardi. He had mentioned once that he liked being a big fish in a small pond. Viscardi offered him the ability to be just that, and he thrived in such an environment. We lost touch when I left Viscardi, but I always wondered what he was up to.

You can imagine my surprise when I got settled at this new campus and saw him whizzing around in his chair. I couldn't believe we were now fifteen and together again in the same place. He still had that bright smile, the charm, and the swagger. He knew it, too. He still got around with the same style wheelchair, but now he had an added accessory. More often than not, he had a basketball on his lap. He had developed a passion for wheelchair basketball, and his skills were incredible! He dribbled, passed, and made three-point shots with one leg while his other leg controlled his power chair. I'm not sure I would have believed it if I hadn't witnessed it myself.

While we both made a handful of other friends that summer, we did most of our activities together. One excursion trip we took was to a Yankees home game. Scott had a wonderful sense of humor, so he thought it would be funny if he wore a hat from the Yankees' hated rivals, the Boston Red Sox. He reasoned that no one would give a kid in a wheelchair with no arms any grief for wearing it. To his surprise and hidden joy, he got roundly booed. That was Scott.

Two months at camp came and went quicker than I would have liked. It was difficult for me to see at the start of that summer that this experience would be a time I needed. Before our parents came to pick us up, Scott and I exchanged numbers and promised to stay in touch. We only lived fifteen minutes away from each other on Long Island, and our parents were very fond of one another, so we had no excuse for not hanging out more. We hugged and I said, "See ya soon!"

A few weeks later, we kept our word, and I went to his house to hang out with him for the day. It was a hot August day and, of course, one of the first things he wanted to do was show off his basketball skills. He needed to practice for an upcoming tournament, so he challenged me to play basketball in his driveway court. I was no match for him. I could barely stand with one crutch and dribble the ball. He was so patient with me, and even when all of my attempted shots were air balls, he made me feel like my effort was valued. He was the captain of his team, and I could see why. He was a competitor at heart but also carried a sense of empathy for others. After schooling me out on his driveway, we went inside for the rest of the afternoon. He showed me how to play his favorite soccer video game then we ate lunch, and his mom even brought us Cold Stone strawberry cheesecake ice cream. It was a day filled with so many laughs, memories, and life lessons that I had no idea I would carry with me to this day.

Shortly before my mom came to get me from his house, we talked about the future. I asked Scotty if he was thinking about going away to college. He told me no, he had a plan. He wanted to find a way to play professional wheelchair basketball. There was only one problem. He used a power chair, and there were no professional teams at the time that would allow him to play because he could be a danger to and hold an advantage against players using manual chairs. He wasn't sure how he was going to make it happen, but he wanted to create more opportunities for players like him. Scotty lived by the mantra, "Failure is not an option." He was inspired to adopt that mantra after falling in love with the song "Lose Yourself," written by Eminem, the rapper. When he set his mind to something, this was the spark that always pushed him forward.

I admired his plan. I told him if anyone was going to figure out a way to make it work, he would. As my mom pulled in the driveway and we said goodbye, he reminded me about a big game he had coming up and invited me to it. I told him we'd try to make it.

I didn't make it. But, for the next few months, we communicated daily through Instant Messenger or in phone calls. I called his house phone one night thinking I was dialing his direct room line, but instead, I had dialed the family line. It was really late at night when his dad answered wondering why we both were still up. It's a memory that makes me laugh now, but in the moment, I was mortified.

Our friendship continued to grow. Our parents got to know each other better, and our afterschool chats continued to be something I looked forward to every day. That all changed when I got an AOL Instant message I wasn't expecting from our mutual friend, Eric.

E: Hey, have you heard about Bubba?

S: No, I just talked to him two days ago. Is he okay?

E: He went to the hospital last night, Steph. He's gone...

There was no way this could be real. I was shattered! I remember looking at the screen feeling so confused. My mom was upstairs, so I screamed as loud as I could, and she came racing down. I asked her to find out if this was actually happening. Eric was one of Scott's best friends, so I knew he wouldn't joke about something like this, but still, it didn't make sense to me. He had just turned sixteen. He was healthy, active, and loved by so many. My mom learned that Scott had suffered a neck aneurysm. There was no association between the aneurysm and his disabilities or any indication that he was in a dangerous health situation. He was there one day, and the next day, he was taken from all of us who loved him way too soon.

I couldn't attend Scotty's funeral, but I did go to his

wake. In the Jewish faith, we don't have wakes, and at fifteen, I was unfamiliar with what the Christian customs were. It was a cold, rainy night in December when I showed up at the wake wearing a bright-pink North Face jacket. I stood out among the dark-clothed line of maybe 1,000 visitors—a testament to Scott's impact on others—who were waiting in line to view the coffin. Worse than that faux pas, I was unprepared to see one of my closest friends lying in an open casket as if he was merely asleep. When it was my turn to view the casket, I gasped aloud and stumbled into his father's arms. His dad caught me and hugged me while I sobbed and sobbed. Through my tears, I promised his dad that I would never let Scotty's legacy die. And I never have. Every event and every competition I participate in I dedicate to Scott's memory, and I proudly embrace his mantra, "Failure is not an option." The reality is that I knew I couldn't carry out Scott's biggest dream of creating a power wheelchair basketball league, but I do strive every day to make a difference for adaptive athletes and to keep his memory alive. I know he'd be proud. Losing someone like Bubba at such a young age taught me how fragile life truly is. He is my guardian angel now, reminding me to push forward and follow my dreams.

CRUMPLED PAPERS AND
A SHATTERED SOUL

I have faced my fair share of adversity and overcome more than most in my mere thirty-two years of life, but if I'm being honest, choosing to write this memoir has been one of the more challenging things I have ever done. Challenging because my story cannot be fully told without sharing my truth, and part of that truth entails exposing very personal, sometimes painful, and traumatic experiences that I have never felt strong enough to share, mostly out of fear. After many years of cognitive behavioral therapy, I came to understand that what I endured as a child, teen, and young adult is, in fact, anything but "normal."

The fear stops here. It's my turn to speak and set this part of me free. I am choosing to share this because no one should ever feel voiceless. This book is a collection of stories that I hope truly empowers you as the reader to look deep within yourself and know that you are capable of way more than you think you are. This story has a happy ending, I promise. Before we get there, though, I'm going to share a part of me that I've been holding onto in silence for too long.

When I got home from my final summer with my siblings at camp, our parents sat us down on the living room couch. Our father had just returned from a business trip to London, and I can clearly remember him handing me a 5ive CD, a British boy band that I really liked. I was so excited! He continued to pass out the souvenirs he had brought home, and then they told us they had an announcement to make. Over the summer, Mom and Dad had chosen to get a divorce. My excitement immediately turned to confusion. From that moment on, my life changed.

My best friend at the time lived five houses down from us, and I would walk to her house almost every day after school and on the weekends. We traded off whose houses we were going to hang out at. So, when my parents broke the news to us, that's exactly where I felt I *needed* to be. I wanted to get out of my house. Life as I knew it had changed without warning, and I didn't like it. As I walked down to her house, I cried. I remember falling into her mom's arms and just feeling sad. This house down the street was my safe place, and I ran straight for it. I didn't know it at the time, but it wouldn't be long before this place I once felt safe in would be the last place I would ever want to be.

As my parents' divorce unfolded, we began shuffling back and forth from house to house. Weekdays with my mom, weekends with our father. At first, it was kind of sweet watching our father try to figure out how to care for the four of us on his own. He would bring in bagels, make pancakes, and even let us paint our rooms whatever color made us happiest. For the first few months, everyone seemed to find a routine, but then he announced he was dating my best friend's mom: the very mom whose arms I sobbed into earlier. It was as though a switch had been flipped in my life, and my father's whole demeanor as a human began to change.

They both changed. You would think it would be great watching our father fall in love again, but it was anything but that. This woman who once made me feel so loved and safe seemed to have changed overnight, making me feel constantly judged and worthless, and sadly, she took our father to the dark side with her. He went from being kind, loving, and supportive to angry, agitated, and annoyed by my very existence. It was such a strange change. I didn't like how he was acting or treating me. I remember asking him one morning while on a walk to my grandparents' synagogue if it was okay if we could continue to have a relationship with just him. He didn't like that that was even a thought and told me no. I'd have to have a relationship with her if I wanted to have any sort of relationship with him. That declaration set the tone for the next twenty years. She had three girls of her own, the oldest one being one of my closest friends, but it became quite clear that that friendship would not last. My father's new relationship moved very quickly, and before we knew it, they were getting married, so now seven kids would be living in the same house on the weekends.

You may be familiar with the Sixties television sitcom, *The Brady Bunch,* and while I would love to say that our lives were like that made-up blended family, it was anything but that. It became very apparent that there were two sets of rules in their house: the rules that her girls had to follow and the rules that *his* children had to follow. Our father no longer had patience; we no longer had conversations that had any sort of substance, and there were no more jokes or trips down memory lane. Our relationship became extremely business-like. When I would try to bring these changes to his attention, I would often get the same response: "I'm not your friend, I am your father, and you will show everyone in this family respect." Our father had a very one-sided view of respect, and I would soon learn that if I did or said anything he didn't agree with, his first reaction was to get angry and instill fear.

As our relationship disintegrated into pieces, I had to watch as he showed fatherly love and affection to three girls he barely knew. There'd be times where we'd be sitting at a family dinner and they'd laugh, talk about their days, and even sit on his lap as he would lovingly rub their backs as he took an interest in the conversation around the table. At first, it made me sad because anytime I would try to insert myself into the conversation, I felt like I was being made fun of or looked down on for my attempts at engagement. There was a clear divide, and it was hard to handle. As the years went on, I dreaded ever having to enter their house. This was not my home, and it was made very clear that I needed to stay in my room and out of the way unless asked to be anywhere else. I was not allowed to have a key to the house or enter through the front door and was certainly not allowed to engage with anyone who the oldest daughter would have over from school. The scare tactic my father used most often was to squeeze my arm and say, "Don't make me smack you," and his wife would grab my face and say something obscene.

I literally felt voiceless. I began to develop anxiety and experienced severe panic attacks. Wednesday nights were when I started feeling anxious, and I would lose two whole days feeling so sick and not wanting to go to that house. All I ever felt was anxiety. I never felt warmth, love, or kindness. I was a burden, and the only reason they tolerated me was because they had to. My father was fond of the saying, "What happens in this house stays in this house," and he and his wife made it clear that there would be dire consequences if we ever tried to talk to or confide in other family members about what was happening at home. Sometimes, I felt as though I was living three different lives: the life I lived at my mom's house, the nonexistent life I lived at their house, and the life I lived in front of everyone else, including my grandparents. It was extremely painful to feel like I was hiding.

To the outside world, it appeared that everything was great. My father was extremely charming to people out in public and even tolerated it when people would rave about me or share in their excitement for something I had done. But, as soon as we were behind closed doors, I became that burden that was just better off not heard or seen.

Life got really dark for me when an altercation with my father got physical. I was about fourteen, and we were all about to go to Israel for a cousin's bar mitzvah. I was told to pack everything I would need about a week before we were to leave. I forgot one thing: the bottom of a two-piece bathing suit. At dinner just before the trip, I was my usual silent self so they wouldn't make me feel stupid when I was asked if everything was packed. I suddenly remembered I had forgotten the bathing suit bottom but promised I would have it packed before we left. My father and his wife both got up from the table. He was red with anger and started screaming at me. He told me to get up, and as I walked to the kitchen, he told his wife to leave because he didn't know what he was going to do to me. She left. He grabbed me by my shirt and started shaking me until I fell to the floor. He threw my crutches down the hall and yelled at me to go to my room. I had to crawl from the kitchen to my room, and when I got behind my bedroom door, I began to shake. I couldn't understand why he was so angry over a piece of clothing. We made the trip to Israel while my anxiety and panic attacks were out of control. I was miserable the entire time. I was hardly acknowledged as being there at all or as a participant on the trip or as being part of the family. His wife even vowed never to take me on another family vacation again, and she kept her word. I never did.

Life was like this for a long time, and the manipulation tactics were overwhelming. I remember when I told my father that Scotty died, and he acted as though he cared. He told me he would call my school to let them know just in case it might affect my day of schoolwork. I thought this was a glimmer of hope that I was actually being shown kindness and that I wouldn't have to hide my feelings and grief. That night, I burst into tears at dinner and was told by my father's wife that if I was going to cry during dinner, I was to go to my room and deal with it but not to do it in front of the family. I didn't understand any of this, but it didn't sit well with me. How could someone who once showed me so much love become so cruel?

I shuttled back and forth from this lonely space for four years until my mom met someone she wanted to spend her life with. This meant yet another change. She met a man who was a widower and who also had three children. That meant that on any given day of the week, there were seven children and two adults living under one roof no matter which house we were in. This situation was largely different in the sense that we all had to get to know each other, but blending our families did not come without its challenges. There were some big differences between the two households, most notably the way we were expected to conduct ourselves. In my father's house, my siblings and I were tightly controlled and treated as second-class citizens. In my mom's house, everything was different, and my time spent there glued me together after weekends of falling apart. Our independence and freedom to be who we were continued just as it had before our parents' divorce. Our new stepdad had a similar relationship with his children, and it made that blended family much easier to accept. Being able to feel like I could breathe made this house better.

My mom is kind and full of good intentions, but our relationship was strained for many years. Early on in the divorce, it felt as if I was made to pick sides between my mom and my father. As a young, impressionable child, I was made to believe the worst about having a good, trusting relationship with my mom. It's sad because as I've grown and am now able to see things a little more clearly, I see that my father was a master at manipulation, and his children paid the greatest price for that.

By my junior year, we moved into a different house with our mom and stepdad and his three children. They only lived a few towns over, so it wasn't a drastic change, but it did mean having to change high schools, and that meant leaving the comfort of my current friends and routine. From middle school through my sophomore year in high school, I had been with the same group of kids. We all knew each other and accepted or ignored one another as part of our routine. Now, I was being thrust into a new environment in unfamiliar territory. I had to start all over again.

Fortunately, my angst was somewhat short-lived when during my first week at the new high school, a girl named Samantha (Sami) befriended me. Sami had a cousin with CP, and she was immediately empathetic to my challenges. She also came from a divorced family, so we were *simpatico* on many levels. I became friends with her family, especially her mother, and she enjoyed a good relationship with my mom. We would often go to each other's houses. We are still close. I was her bridesmaid at her wedding, and her kids call me Aunt Stephie. I am amazed by how often what appears to be a difficult upcoming situation in life results in a beautiful, lifelong friendship. In that way, I am blessed.

I had always enjoyed being in school, and I think part of that was because I found myself gravitating toward adults who not only made me feel seen but heard. I found myself confiding in teachers and guidance counselors throughout my most formative years and, to this day, I credit these relationships for keeping me focused because they taught me to celebrate my successes. One individual who deserves more credit than he will ever be willing to accept is Brian.

Brian was my middle school guidance counselor. He was always positive, calm, professional, and had a wonderful way of making me feel believed. As life got more challenging, mostly from my parents' divorce, Brian supported me and gave me a safe place to express my feelings. I trusted and confided in him. That relationship continued from middle school to high school and on through college, and he is still a part of my life. He has always encouraged me to advocate for myself and for other students, especially those with disabilities. We would talk about my feelings often and, as life got more complex, he would help guide me in the best ways he knew how. I remember feeling like no one understood me when Scott died, and when I had learned that Brian had lost his best friend Sean at a young age, I felt I had finally found an adult who understood. Meeting Brian at eleven years old, I had no idea of the positive impact this person was going to have on my life but, over the last twenty-one years, his support, guidance, and genuine care for my well-being has helped shape me into the person I am. I will forever be grateful for the adults who made me feel like my voice mattered.

As sad as I was not being able to see some of the friends and teachers I had known since middle school, going to the new high school also meant I could have a fresh start. It let me breathe a little more knowing that school could be my safe place where I didn't have to worry about running into my father or any of his new family every single day of the week. But that wasn't enough to overcome the constant anxiety and depression I was feeling as I shuttled from my mother's house to my father's.

We would leave my father's house on Sunday nights, and as soon as I'd cross the threshold into my mom's house, it was like the hourglass full of sand got flipped upside-down. I had two and a half full days of enjoyment and then on Wednesday night, like clockwork, the panic would set in because Friday was just around the corner. That's when I began confiding in my aunt about my building anxiety. She understood the family dynamic in a way no one else could. We began speaking two or three times a day.

Sometimes, I just wanted to hear her voice. She was kind, gentle, and was never once judgmental. She would let me talk about the same thing over and over and never made me think my feelings were invalid. I credit her patience, kindness, and love for the reason I'm still here today. My anxiety had turned into full-fledged daily panic attacks; I felt like I could never do anything right, and I remember one night thinking how quiet it must feel when you die.

I thought that people around me would have a much simpler, better quality of life if I just ended my own. This was the darkest, scariest corner my brain had ever gone to. I thought about the different ways I could do it and then, during one of the many conversations with my aunt, I told her what I was thinking. Instead of reacting harshly or not believing me, she spent most of her night and the next day calling me, reminding me of how loved I was and telling me how she was going to help me find my way out of this very dark place. She did. I never once questioned her love or if I could trust her. She taught me the importance of finding a good therapist and what it meant to want to truly live life to the fullest. And she saved my life.

Through therapy and my blossoming relationship with my aunt, I learned that writing was one outlet that could give my voice power and greater meaning. I used to write a lot in my teens. I wrote whenever inspiration struck. It was a way for me to express myself without fear or judgment. I loved the way people reading my poems or creative works would react to what they were reading, so when I was seventeen, I thought writing a poem would be a great way to express my feelings about my relationship with my father. I wrote it in part for my own solace and in part as a last-ditch effort at getting him to see who I was and what we had become. When I gave it to him, he read a few lines, crumpled it, and threw it in the trash. That symbolically told me all I needed to know. Our relationship as I once knew it was gone.

My relationship with my father has barely cracked

the surface since I was eighteen years old. To the outside world, he's done a lot of good, and for some, that may very well be true. For me, for many years, I went along with this charade hoping things would change. If only I did something different, achieved more success, or acted differently, he might actually treat me with kindness. The sad part is that I now know there's nothing I could have done or said. A few years ago, I sat across from him, face to face, sharing how hurt I felt and what I needed in order to move forward. I needed him to own his actions, the pain he caused, and the damage he did. Unfortunately, he could not do any of this. In return, I learned a significant lesson: *I am way more powerful than I give myself credit for.* The moment he decided to dismiss his past actions was the moment I decided to take greater control of my future. It was my turn to speak, but my words had fallen on deaf ears. There was nothing more to say other than *I'm done.*

It is My Turn to Speak (2007)

I apologize, but I have something to say.

You need to stop for a minute and just listen.

For once, it is my turn to tell you what would make me happy.

You scream and yell, but the message never stays put.

Only able to take so much before being destroyed.

It hurts to know on the surface everything is gone:

your hugs, kisses, and even kind words.

It's actually pathetic that all of that has disappeared.

I find humor in the fact that you have no voice of your own.

You live vicariously through someone who has completely destroyed you.

I am disrespectful?

I should learn to be a decent human being?

I should try to build a relationship?

These suggestions are made in almost every conversation, but little do you know about me.

Disrespect to you is not speaking to the person who ruined each decent thing about you.

Being a decent human being is making you aware of things I know you don't truly care for.

And building a relationship is like building a castle made of sand:

For a minute aesthetically appealing, but it's easily destroyed by a few drops of water.

I take it back.

My apology is not for having something to say.

My apology is for you to hold onto.

You say you are done with me.

One day, you will realize I was done a long time ago.

For once, it is my turn to tell you what would make me happy.

Take a look at yourself.

The mirror you have been staring at is fogged almost completely.

Take a minute to clear it off.

Look at yourself.

I miss that person.

I know who he is.

He is the person who made his little girl happy.

That little girl is all grown up,

About to leave, and truly never wants to look back.

Years and years, I have taken all of this,

Your actions and words stuffed deep in my heart.

You can never take them back because I have

them now.

I have always had my voice,

The strongest part of who I am.

So for once, just listen,

Please listen.

It is my turn to speak.

FINDING MY TRUE VOICE

During my junior year in high school, I took a trip with my father and twin brother to Lynn University in Boca Raton, Florida. When you pull up to the university, there is a long driveway leading to an enormous roundabout. The roundabout is filled with flags representing all of the countries of the attending students. At the time of my visit, there were ninety-three country flags. We met with an admissions advisor and took a tour of the campus, and I knew immediately that this was where I was going to attend college.

During my visit to Lynn, one of the last stops on the tour was the bookstore. Before leaving, I chose one item to remember this experience by. I purchased a brown sweatshirt with "Lynn University" printed on the front in light-pink lettering. I was that certain this was soon going to be my new home. I wore that sweatshirt constantly because it was comfortable but also because it was my way of manifesting my future acceptance. I had applied to college between my junior and senior years of high school.

I remember it being a windy October day in New York. I was wearing my Lynn sweatshirt when I went outside the school to make a phone call on my lunch break. It had been a few weeks since I'd faxed the requested application documents over to the university, so I called the Lynn University health office to be sure my medical records had been received with my application because they came from different origins. I spoke to a nurse there, and she said they had been received. Then she said, "Congratulations on your acceptance." I was a bit stunned because I had never received an acceptance letter or any packet about attending the university or what would be expected. The nurse transferred the call to admissions, and they confirmed that I had been accepted. A week or so later, I received the official acceptance letter. I was the first senior in my class to be accepted to a university and know where I was headed after graduation. I still had state exams to pass before graduating, so I couldn't completely check out, but I felt a huge weight off my shoulders knowing I had a plan in place for after high school. I had determined where I was going to college before I had even applied. I actually applied to two colleges, Lynn and Nova Southeastern University in Davie, Florida. I chose Lynn for my undergraduate education and ended up going to Nova for my master's.

As the seasons began to change and the end of the school year was right around the corner, I began thinking about prom. Many of my friends were coupled up and I didn't really have any prospects to count on, so I began to become comfortable with the idea that I probably wouldn't be going to prom. I was okay with that. That was until I was chatting with my friend Steve, who I had met the summer before at a punk rock concert. He was the drummer in a local band, and after the concert was over, we had ended up chatting for a few hours and began an awesome friendship. He was very attractive, a little bit older than me, and lived a few towns away. When I told him that I was probably not going to go to prom, he insisted that I go with him. It was a very kind gesture, and I accepted.

I went dress shopping with my grandma and my mom. It was such a fun experience and, after much trial and error, we found the most gorgeous dress. It was a very sparkly, dark-grey dress with a baby-pink lining, and it made me feel so beautiful (I think I might have worn that dress eight more times after prom). I had found the perfect dress, a beautiful purse to match, and even had a hot date. I didn't think I would be excited about going to prom, but it turns out I was.

A few hours before Steve arrived to pick me up, I had my hair, nails, and makeup done. I received the full preprom pampered experience and truly felt beautiful. My grandparents and my uncle stopped by my mom's house to see me and my brother all dressed up and to take a few pictures. In most movies and TV shows, people take a limo to prom. Not us. Steve pulled up to my house in a grey, drop-top BMW convertible. I was shocked. He came inside the house, offered me a wrist corsage, and chatted with everyone before my family took a few more pictures.

It was customary to go to a friend's house before prom and take pictures as a group. For us, that meant Sami's house. We loaded up in Steve's car and drove to Sami's to take about a thousand more pre-prom pictures. Once we ran out of poses and time, we were finally ready to attend senior prom. The prom was full of music, dancing, and so many laughs. Initially, I had been okay with missing out on this rite of passage, but I'm so glad I decided to go because that dress and those memories I will cherish forever. After high school, Steve joined the military and we lost touch, though we have kept up with each other through Facebook.

Graduation was just three days after prom. This was a huge accomplishment considering it wasn't a sure thing that I would make it out of the NICU let alone graduate high school and be heading off to an out-of-state university in the fall.

***

Lynn University is a small private school. When I hear people say college is the best four years of your life, I agree. But for me, my time at Lynn consisted of more student leadership opportunities than late-night ragers or Greek life parties. The thing I loved most about Lynn was the family feel. Because the school was so small, it felt as though everyone knew each other within the first week. Lynn also had a very small Greek life presence consisting of only two fraternities and one sorority. At first, I was drawn to Greek life because it seemed like the best way to get involved and socialize, but it didn't take long to realize it wasn't really my thing. I enjoyed my experience but being surrounded by a bunch of girls all the time, there was no way to avoid drama, and ultimately, the experience was not as positive as I would have hoped.

After freshman year, I decided to leave the sorority and instead began to learn all about student leadership and dedicated my off time to helping put on campus events.

The first student leadership meeting I attended was a Monday night Residence Hall Association (RHA) meeting. RAs were fellow students placed in a leadership role to look after the well-being of the students who resided in their residence halls. RHA meetings gave the students who weren't in these leadership roles an opportunity to use their voices to help better the overall campus living experience.

After my very first meeting, I felt I would be a good representative for students with disabilities and a positive voice for their specific needs. During these meetings, I would advocate for my needs as well as those of the adaptive community at large. It was an extremely empowering feeling and helped me gain an enormous amount of confidence as I continued to navigate my very first year on this new campus.

During my first year on campus, I discovered that I was one of a handful of students who used accessibility devices to independently navigate the campus. I took it upon myself to be the one who was willing to speak up when something wasn't working for us or needed improvement. Fortunately, the administrative staff was more than willing to listen to what I had to say. For example, many automatic doors on campus weren't always working, so after I brought it up to the administration, they had somebody walk around the whole campus with me to check every single button at least once a month to make sure they were all working well and students were able to use the buttons to automatically open the doors as intended—a small thing unless you use crutches or a wheelchair, or are otherwise encumbered.

I would continue to attend Student Government Association (SGA) meetings to ensure that my voice was being heard, and the coolest part was that I never felt like any of my concerns fell on deaf ears. The university staff and my fellow students made me feel like my voice and opinions had true value. SGA meetings happened weekly and, as I attended more of them to be sure I was staying up to date on what was happening on campus, I got an opportunity to propose a campus-wide event that would recognize Disability Awareness Month. My initial proposal was accepted and, to my surprise, the students seemed really excited about it. I proposed four big campus events that the students, faculty, and staff could participate in. I put together a team of friends who helped me execute the events and found a way to inject even more meaning into the month by raising money for The Bubba Fund throughout the month in honor of my dear friend Scotty.

In October 2009, Disability Awareness Month (DAM) debuted at Lynn. The four main events were:

- A week using a wheelchair

- A disability-themed movie

- A different abilities dinner

- A wheelchair basketball tournament

Each activity was a learning experience available to anyone who wanted to be part of it. We convinced local medical supply companies to donate the wheelchairs that people would be sitting in for a week and the basketball chairs used during the basketball tournament.

During the "week using a wheelchair" event, participants were asked to try their best to navigate the school as if they needed to use a wheelchair every day. Obviously, there were going to be some exceptions like getting up to go to the restroom or getting out if their residence hall had no accessible options, but one of the most remarkable things I noticed was that when we would meet up at the end of the day to discuss the experience, the participants would note things about the campus' accessibility or challenges they never truly thought about until they were forced to. The president of the university even committed to spending his day using a chair, and when the day was done, he admitted that the campus was pretty accessible but definitely had things that could use improvement.

The different abilities dinner took place in the dining hall, and we gave students the option to eat their meal a few different ways:

- Blindfolded

- One hand tied behind their back

- With earplugs

- Muted

This experience went better than I could have ever

imagined. People took it so seriously and learned a lot about different ways to communicate with one another while sharing a meal regardless of ability. To me, this was a beautiful thing to witness.

The movie I decided to show, *Murder Ball,* is about a group of wheelchair rugby players who are extremely passionate about the sport and live pretty amazing independent lives. The movie screening was a hit, and I think it helped people develop a greater understanding of just how much is possible when you have a support system and a positive mindset.

We saved the wheelchair basketball tournament for last because I thought it could be a great way to have some fun, celebrate all that we had accomplished, and honor Scott's legacy. I was blown away by how excited students and faculty were about this game. We had done some local marketing to Florida Atlantic University across the street and, to my surprise, they committed to fielding three full teams.

Because I knew absolutely nothing about wheelchair basketball other than being schooled by Bubba, I hired someone to come in, teach the participants about the game, and run the tournament. It was an amazing experience. We raised a ton of money as well as awareness.

In recognition of my involvement in so many student activities, I was awarded Female Student Leader of the Year. I was also nicknamed Madam Mayor by professor and author Dr. Robert Watson.

Over the four years I was there, I can wholeheartedly say that the Lynn staff tried their best to continue to evolve with the times. I'm proud to say that twelve years later, Disability Awareness Month is still a staple at Lynn. It's amazing to know that something that started out as a small idea turned into a recurring tradition on campus.

My biggest challenge at the university wasn't the schoolwork or getting around or social challenges. I fit in very naturally. The main challenge came in the form of one of the university administrators. But, like many of my challenges, my answer to it helped solidify my belief in myself while making a difference for those who followed me.

During sophomore year, I developed a friendship with a staff member who was my mentor, Annie. Annie and another faculty member lead a study abroad program, usually during the winter term. The selected students would study one particular subject matter. My passions were in leadership and student development, and I was fortunate enough to be selected to participate in the program in January 2010.

That year's trip was scheduled to be in New Zealand, the farthest I have ever been outside of the U.S. I was excited to go, though a bit concerned about how I would raise the $5,000 cost of the trip. Enter my wonderfully, continually supportive grandparents—there for me again to make this happen. But my elation was soon cut short when I was unexpectedly called to the office of the vice-president of academic affairs, Cynthia. When I rolled into the office in my power chair, I was confronted by a large conference room with about six people seated around it, Cynthia, sitting to my right, began with small talk then asked me if I knew why I was there.

"No, ma'am, I don't know," I said.

"I don't think it is safe for you to go on the New Zealand trip unless you have the help of an aide," she responded as if we were still discussing the new hall paint.

I hadn't had an aide since the end of middle school. When I asked her why I needed an aide, she said for my safety and the safety of the other students. She then indicated that it was Annie who said she would feel safer if I had an aide. (I knew there was no truth to that statement.) Annie, cognizant of the need to protect her job, remained silent. Unbeknownst to Cynthia and the others, Annie and I had developed a wonderful friendship. I knew she was willing to do anything we needed to in order for us to have a successful travel experience together so, I understood her silence. Before going on this trip, Cynthia reprimanded her for inviting a student with a disability. Annie argued that she believed inviting students, regardless of their abilities, was part of her job, but Cynthia did not budge.

I argued with Cynthia for a bit, insisting that I knew what I needed best. I could tell she did not like me advocating for myself. And then she said it. She said it dead to my face: "I know when you look at yourself you don't see a wheelchair, but when I look at you, Stephanie, I see a chair."

There was a rush of potential responses that ran through my brain, none of them particularly eloquent. I settled for holding it in and letting the upset in my face

speak for me. Cynthia, unmoved and completely uncon-
cerned with her ignorance, gave me an ultimatum: Either take an aide on the trip or stay home. I wasn't going
to be defeated and denied by this woman, so I went on
the trip with an aide. No disrespect to the aide, but she
did nothing for me. How could she? She wasn't needed.

I spent a good deal of my time traveling around New
Zealand with Annie and, at other times, with the entire
group of fifteen students. On one particular day, we all
went to Taupo, home of the Taupo swing on New Zealand's highest clifftop. The swing is located one hundred
and fifty-four feet above Waikato River, and we were
there to bungee jump from that Taupo swing: fourteen
able-bodied students and one who doesn't see a wheelchair.

Now, I am not drawn to heights at all, excepting my
time on the trapeze, but some part of me saw that bungee jump as a "screw you" to Cynthia. (Don't judge.) To
get to the top, you had to climb about eighty steps. I was
able to pull myself up using the rails and not my crutches
with one of the site's adventure guides following behind
me—just in case. The other tourists on their tours took
pictures of me making this difficult ascent and urged me
on with shouts of "you go" along the way. I like to think
I was motivating some of them and not just inspiring
them.

It likely took me about twelve minutes to reach the
top. That meant I had roughly twelve minutes to rethink
screwing Cynthia (so to speak) and head back down, but I
persevered. I got to the top super nervous about the height

and what was still awaiting me but excited at the same time. When it was my turn for the swing, I was strapped for safety to one of the guides, who kept telling me, "Open your eyes, open your eyes." But I was so scared, it took a few minutes before I dared. The view of the river below from one hundred and fifty-four feet above was breathtaking. Sitting on that swing, about to be released through the air, was also breathtaking—in a very different and real way. Whoosh... Before I could protest, we were bungee jumping down to within inches of the water then springing back up, and then down again, and then being pulled back up to the platform to disembark. I can't say for certain that I would do it again, but I can tell you that I didn't stop flying until long after that jump.

As it happens, I was close to the president of the college and also a blogger for the university website. When I returned from New Zealand, I blogged about the meeting with Cynthia and my trip. Shortly after that, the university president called me into his office. I thought he was going to reprimand me and have me take the post down. Instead, and to my surprise and relief, he told me not to take it down, and he apologized for Cynthia's behavior. I told him that I didn't need an apology but that I believed she had no right to talk to a student like that and that she didn't belong as part of the campus community culture. A few weeks later, she was gone.

***

After the success of all of my student advocate activities, I started to dive more fully into being a student leader on campus. My days were filled with classes and assignments, and many of my nights were filled with stress over exams, but I felt like I was attending more organizational meetings than classes. I had gotten so deeply involved with taking care of everyone around me that it took me a while to realize that I had forgotten how important it was to take care of myself. I gained the freshman fifteen (fifteen pounds of weight), and when I saw my image on Facebook, I didn't immediately recognize myself.

After that realization, I had a conversation with my grandpa about wanting to find a personal trainer. He agreed to pay for a trainer as long as I stuck with it. I told him I would, and with that agreement, I began to search for a trainer. After a few Google searches and a couple of phone calls, I connected with a local trainer named Frank. He had some experience working with people with CP, and after talking with him about my goals, I called my grandpa and told him I had found someone to work with. Because he was going to be paying for this person's services, he told me that he and my grandma were going to fly to Florida for a day to meet Frank in person. On one hand, this was surprising because my grandparents always joked about how much they disliked the state of Florida, and to come for just a day was a lot of effort but it was also yet another example of their unconditional love and support.

My grandparents and Frank picked a day and agreed to meet for lunch. During this lunch, my grandparents were very impressed with Frank and agreed on a price for his training services. And so began my personal training session with Frank.

During our first training session, I showed Frank all the things I was able to do such as walking with my crutches, walking on the treadmill at slow speed, a few weightlifting machine exercises, and how I moved from one place to the next independently. After my first "athlete" assessment, he asked me to think about a tangible goal we could work toward. Immediately, weight loss came to mind. He told me to think outside that box. My body was going to change, we were going to work on making those changes, and he wanted me to dig deeper. I told him I needed a few days to think about it and promised him that by our next session, I would have a more meaningful answer.

I went back to campus and happened to bump into one of the lead RAs. His name was Jon, and he was a fitness enthusiast who loved to run. When I say he loved to run, I mean he'd run at least ten miles a day for fun. I was so excited to tell Jon about my first training session because I knew he would genuinely appreciate it. After hearing my excitement, he asked if I'd like to come to a race taking place that weekend to cheer him on as he ran a local 10K. Jon had always been supportive of me, so this was a no-brainer. I told him I'd love to support him and that I'd be there with bells on.

The morning of Jon's race, I got there early to be certain I had a good seat to see him start the race. To my surprise, I saw a handful of empty wheelchairs to the left of the start. *What are all those chairs doing here...just empty?* Then I saw that a few feet behind the starting line was a group of individuals on handcycles warming up for the race. It was the first time I'd ever seen people in the adaptive population as part of a "running" event. I had no idea this was even a possibility. These adaptive athletes started their race about five minutes before the runners. I learned that they do this for safety reasons so that the athletes on handcycles don't get trampled by a stampede of enthusiastic bipeds (makes sense).

As I watched the handcyclists make their way to the starting line, Frank's assignment popped into my head. *Could I race? Would this be something I would be good at?* As the event began, the athletes weren't the only racers; my mind was racing, and I really wanted to get some answers. I saw Jon right before his start. He was excited to see me, greeted me with a hug, and thanked me for showing up. Before he left to get warmed up, I asked him if he'd ever seen that group of handcyclists before. He said yes and pointed to a table with a banner that read: Achilles International. It was a team of handcycling athletes who all had physical disabilities. Jon told me that they came to a lot of races and had many chapters around the country. I was intrigued. I thanked John for the answer and wished him luck in his race. I told him I would see him at the finish line and that I hoped he'd have a lot of fun.

After watching Jon run off into the distance from the start line, I walked around and gravitated toward the table he had pointed out. I went over and happened to see the director of the South Florida chapter. His name was Chris, and he seemed very excited when I showed interest in his program. He was a quadriplegic himself and told me they were looking for more females for his team. I told him I had CP, and he looked at me and said, "That doesn't matter; you look strong. I think you'd do really well on a handcycle."

After sharing my full name with him, he asked me if I was any relation to another Hammerman he knew. I smiled and told him that I did but that I usually just called him Grandpa. *Of course he knew Grandpa.* It was no surprise that my grandparents would be involved with a program like this; I was just surprised that I happened to connect with this group by accident. Chris didn't waste any time asking me if I wanted to hop on a handcycle and go for a spin. I told him I did but that I needed to be at the race finish line because my friend was running and I had come to the event specifically to cheer him on. He understood and told me he would look for me at the table again after the competitors completed the race.

Jon was an extremely accomplished athlete, known in South Florida for some of the fastest finishing times. Back on campus, his office walls were decorated with racing bibs and medals, and he would soon add another set to add to his already impressive collection. I quickly made my way to the finish line because I knew it wouldn't be long before he'd be crossing it. I can't remember his finish time, but it was no surprise to me to see that he had placed among the top three runners out of hundreds. Once he'd collected himself after crossing the finish line, we shared a high-five, and I eagerly told him who I had spoken to and asked him if he wanted to make his way back to that table with me.

When Chris saw us approach, he gestured us toward him. He was seated in his wheelchair with a handcycle parked in front of him. "This one may not be an exact fit for you, but let's get you on this bike," he said. "I think you're going to love it. If you do, I'll be sure you get a bike specifically ordered for your needs." Jon helped me get into the bike, safely strapped me in, and then Chris instructed me on how to move it. Both hands rotated away from my body to propel the bike forward. I did a few slow rotations, learned how to access the brake, and then took a spin around the display area. It was similar to being in the pool; I felt strong, free, and in control. I spun back around toward Chris, and I couldn't believe what he said to me as I stopped in front of him: "Ten months from now, you are going to do a marathon with us in Palm Beach!" *Um, excuse me...what?*

I laughed at him. There was no way he was serious. He looked at me, reiterated how strong I was, and said that this could be a lot of fun. He wanted me on the team. It didn't cost anything; I just had to want to do it and train.

That became my goal for Frank. I'd showed up to a 10K to support a friend, and now I was leaving the event having joined a handcycle team and committing to doing a full marathon in just ten months. When I broke the news to Frank, I thought he was going to say I was certifiably insane, but to my surprise, he was extremely proud and supportive!

With Frank's support of my now tangible goal and

Chris's willingness to help me get the right bike for me, I was completely motivated to start training for this race. While we were waiting for the bike to arrive, we started working on my cardiovascular endurance. I walked on my crutches in almost every session that we had together, and when I wasn't using my crutches, he had me on the treadmill at a slow and controlled pace. Once the bike came in and I was fitted and ready to ride, we started taking some of our training sessions on the road. Frank would ride his bike alongside mine to make sure that I was staying safe and that I felt comfortable. We started out with short-distance training, but as my endurance got stronger, we increased the distance. When I wasn't working with Frank or working on my schoolwork or attending student leadership meetings, I found enjoyment in going to spin classes.

Flywheel Sports spin studio classes were the newest and hottest cycling classes. Most people with a physical disability probably wouldn't look at spin as a viable option, but I'm not "most people," and the worst that somebody could say was "no." I had purchased an indoor trainer for my bike so that I could safely train when I didn't have somebody to ride with me, so it didn't seem like too much to ask the staff at Flywheel if I could bring my bike and trainer into the class. I wanted to take the class like any other athlete.

The staff had never had somebody like me asking to do such a thing or even be in a spin class, so for them, this was a new experience as well—but to my delight, they were accommodating and welcoming. They made it such a fun experience.

My time at Flywheel introduced me to some of the most wonderful people. Don, one of the first instructors I worked with, was someone I immediately felt comfortable with. I learned a lot from him. He had never worked with a handcyclist before, but he had worked as a guide for blind athletes during triathlons, so he had a little more experience working with somebody in the adaptive population than other trainers. He never treated me any differently than the other athletes. He learned how my bike worked, how the resistance worked, and how far he could push me as an athlete. I took his classes at least three to four times a week. I became quite addicted to spin classes and just spending time on my bike. Little by little, Frank started seeing a lot of improvement in my movement as well. I had changed my nutrition to match my training schedule and was becoming a lot happier as I continued to focus on my health and well-being. Between my time with Frank and my time at Flywheel, I was able to handle so much more when it came to building my endurance and the amount of distance I was able to go at one time. There were some days when I would even take back-to-back classes just to make sure that I was ready for the amount of work that was going to be necessary to complete a full marathon. For those that don't know, a full marathon distance is 26.2 miles, and for someone who had never even thought about going more than two miles, this was a huge adjustment.

As the time went on and the race got closer, I became more confident. I would meet with Chris and some of the team members to practice maybe once a month, and it was amazing to see how everyone treated each other. It wasn't about who used what accessibility device or what disability they had; it was all about being seen as an athlete and being taken seriously. About five months before the race, I told my family what I was training for and, just like with Frank, I thought they were all going to think I was absolutely insane. And just as with Frank, everybody was extremely supportive—so much so that they planned to come down to Florida for the race (*no pressure*).

Before I knew it, Frank and I had put the final touches on our training plan, and I was getting ready for race weekend. As promised, my whole family came down to Florida to support me, and my grandparents went so far as to host a dinner the night before the race for all of the athletes. After the dinner ended, Chris held a team meeting to make sure that everybody was ready for the day ahead. We had to get up very early and be at the start line at 5:30 a.m. Our bikes would be loaded into a trailer that would meet us at the start line in the morning. We learned all about the course details, went over safety precautions, and learned about the volunteers who were going to be racing alongside us. Chris knew this was going to be a very important day for me, so he decided to forego personally participating in the competition and race alongside me.

I barely slept that night, and when I woke up the next morning, I was full of adrenaline and butterflies. I could barely eat but a few bites of some oatmeal and a banana. Making my way to the start line felt surreal; less than a year ago, this was nowhere on my radar, and now I had a new goal—complete a full marathon. I knew I wasn't going to be the fastest or the one with the most experience, but I was so excited to just have some fun. I wasn't certain how this was going to go or how long it was going to take, but I was going to do everything in my power to finish.

My whole family had made shirts with my face on them! The front of the shirt had a picture of me from the first 5K I ever did, and the back took my breath away. "Failure is not an option," as Scott Pollock always said. This was the exact motivation I needed.

December 4, 2011, is a day I will never forget. It took 4:34:16 for me to become a competitive athlete. Covering 26.2 miles on a handcycle was no joke. I remember looking down at my hands, which were all ripped up; they were bloody and dirty. Then I looked at the clock and just knew that I could do better. Then I looked to Chris. And smiled. He had told me before the race that this might be my first race but certainly wouldn't be my last. He was right.

After the race, Frank and I worked together for a few more months. I had grown to have a deep connection with Frank and was so grateful for the time that he had taken out of his life to impact mine, but I also knew that I was searching for a new challenge. When I shared my thoughts with Frank, he completely understood; we had been working together for over a year when we decided it was time to end our working relationship.

I handcycled for another year and a half with Achilles International of South Florida. A year later, after so many more miles under my belt, I competed in the same marathon. I had so much more confidence and experience and was still having a lot of fun. I took my time down to 3:22:19. That time signaled to me that I had become an athlete, and I decided it was time to hang up my helmet. It sounds crazy, but I wanted to end my racing career on a high note and knew there were newer, bigger opportunities for me to have a positive impact on the adaptive community soon. And then I found CrossFit.

IGNITING THE SPARK

Completing my first full marathon was the catalyst to finding my greater purpose. Once I crossed that finish line, it was as if I had been introduced to a part of me that I had never met. It was that day that I realized I wanted to tap into my athletic ability and dive deeper into the things my body was capable of doing.

I went back to work with my trainer for a few weeks, but boredom was setting in. It was the same routine almost every day. A few minutes walking on the treadmill, a couple sets on a weight machine, then back to the treadmill. This rinse-and-repeat cycle was great and helped create a rock-solid foundation when it came to consistency. But I just knew that I wanted to be challenged by something more than consistency in order to continue to see progress as an athlete.

Our college dining hall was the one place during the day where staff members and students had the opportunity to sit and socialize. I had become friendly with Jesse, one of our volleyball coaches. Jesse was very passionate about the sport she coached, but she was also passionate about staying fit and active in the offseason and, as we spoke about how I was feeling about training, she invited me to visit her CrossFit gym and check it out. I had never heard of this type of training. When I got home, I did a quick Google search. At first glance, it looked like if you did this type of workout, you would become very strong. I saw pictures of both men and women with a ton of muscles and incredible-looking physiques lifting heavy barbells and swinging from gymnastic rings. I quickly realized this was something that piqued my interest. I didn't see anyone like me in any of the photos or videos that had come up in the search results, and I think that's why I was so drawn to wanting to learn more about this gym and the Crossfit program. I might not be lifting very heavy weights or swinging from rings anytime soon, but I wouldn't know what I was capable of doing if I didn't at least show up and try. I was definitely nervous, but I knew I needed to get uncomfortable in order to continue being challenged. I was driven by the thought of making a change and excited about the possibility of opening a new door for others who might do that same Google search; I wanted to be someone they could relate to. It was a tall order, but I knew deep down that I was ready for whatever the outcome might be. The first thing I had to do was show up at the CrossFit gym.

May 3, 2012 was the day I decided to show up. I drove myself to the gym, sat in my power chair, placed my crutches across my lap, and rolled right up to an open garage door. The morning class was just ending. Some people were high-fiving one another, and others were laying on their backs breathing hard and sweating profusely but with big smiles on their faces. You could tell they felt a sense of accomplishment. It was a little intimidating to see in person their muscular resemblance to the pictures I saw on the internet. However, after spending about fifteen minutes observing them, I felt as though I would fit in because I loved a good challenge.

The societal perception is that someone like me, a wheelchair user with CP, wouldn't be able to do something as intense as CrossFit. This is why I was so drawn to the idea of trying this new way of approaching fitness. It was true that I might not be approaching each movement in the traditional sense, but I was going to do everything I could to see how I could help change people's perceptions.

A few people said hello as they collected their things or were wiping down equipment. No one seemed shocked or scared that I had rolled into their space. It seemed as though they knew that if I was there, I must be ready to experience what this community had to offer.

Once the athletes had left the building, a very muscular man approached me, extended his hand, and with a very noticeable New York accent, said, "Hi there, I'm Scott, but everyone calls me 'Turbo.' Welcome to the Garage." We shook hands, and then I launched into a short explanation of why I had shown up that day.

"Hey, Turbo! I'm Steph," I began. "I'm a competitive handcyclist with cerebral palsy, and I'm looking to find something that will make me stronger and faster. I've never done CrossFit before, but I'd really like to try."

"Well, Steph, nice to meet you. I have never worked with anyone with CP before, so this would be new territory for me as well. I guess we will be learning together."

That was my in. The door was wide open—my first opportunity to experience the change I needed. We spent about twenty minutes talking about my goals, my movement capabilities, and my challenges, and once he felt he understood my unique qualities, Turbo put me to work.

The CrossFit methodology is all about functional movement and preparing you for life's realities such as picking yourself up off the floor safely and effectively. Movements like the "deadlift" (picking weight up off the floor) and the "strict press" (moving weight from your shoulders and pressing it straight over head) can be applied to picking a bag of groceries up off the floor or trying to put a heavy pot in an overhead cabinet. This sport has many different movements that are put into practice in everyday life. One movement that is almost universal in CrossFit is the burpee.

The burpee is a classic functional movement people love to hate, and it couldn't be any more relevant to me and my independence. A burpee simply involves dropping face-down to the floor and getting back up to an upright position.

Turbo asked me if I'd ever done one. When I said no, he proceeded to show me what a rep looked like. He got down on the floor, laying flat on his stomach, and within three seconds he'd popped himself back up to an upright position. He made it look effortless.

"I want you to put yourself on the floor and get back up."

In my head, that task seemed simple enough, but in reality, it took a lot more effort than one would think.

First, I would have to lower myself to the ground and lie flat, then I would have to get back up again. Try it without using your legs. I dare you!

I leaned on my crutches and slowly bent my knees until they approached and then safely landed on the mat. I was halfway there. At first, I held my crutches tightly in my hands, afraid to let go of the security they afforded me and afraid I might fall forward on my face. But then I realized they would have to go if I was going to complete the move. Then, I heard Turbo say in the most endearing way possible, "Now, get the fuck up." It made me laugh, but I did what he said, and I began to get myself up.

My body was fighting spasticity. Every time I would press up to start to get to my hands and knees, my legs would kick back out from under me, forcing me to lay back down. It took several attempts before I got the right rhythm, and I was finally able to get back up to a kneeling position. Once I had accomplished that, I grabbed my crutches and, using the strength I had garnered from handcycling, pushed myself up to a standing position. Success!

The whole process took about twenty-five minutes from down to up. For perspective, keep in mind that it took Turbo three to five seconds. My time was not exactly a record, but once I was standing upright, I felt a sense of accomplishment. It was one of the toughest things I had done in a long time, and I knew I had made a great decision by choosing to show up. This was going to be challenging and a lot of fun.

Turbo was patient and encouraging but never coddling. We both agreed that hopping into a class setting right away was going to be tough, so we decided on a three-times-a-week schedule to begin testing things one on one.

I left that day feeling great. I left that day feeling like I had an opportunity and an obligation to break down barriers and any stereotypes or perceptions there might be about someone with CP lifting weights. Little by little, Turbo and I created an indelible bond. I would try mimicking CrossFit movements to the best of my ability, and if it worked, he would film it to track my progress.

It was amazing to feel my confidence growing week after week and to realize that I was capable of doing way more than I ever believed I could when I first entered that garage. My burpees began getting faster, and I was learning how to handle objects like kettlebells, barbells, and wall balls safely and effectively. One thing that we worked on a lot that was a constant struggle, though, was jumping.

Jumping is an explosive movement, and I quickly learned that to experience a similar stimulus, I would have to hold onto a bar. That's when the concept of "adapting" truly came into play. Not everything was going to look the same as it would when performed by an able-bodied person, but we began slightly changing movements to work within my abilities at the time. With every adaptation came trial, error, and success. With that success came a sense of confidence and a desire to want to be challenged further.

Our sessions became routine. Monday, Wednesday, and Friday, I had one hour with Turbo. In that hour, I was like a sponge, soaking up as much knowledge and experience as I could. As this became part of my routine, we began to document it: photos, videos, successes, and even failed attempts at movements. Social-media platforms were pretty new at the time, so I was lucky if my first few pieces of content reached at most fifty people. As I began posting more consistently, though, my following began to increase, and people started sharing my videos and interacting with me through comments and direct messages. The word "inspirational" got thrown around a lot, and it still does, but the messages that truly made me realize I was making an impact were from others with CP or the parents of kids with CP. They told me how grateful they were to see this kind of content because it helped them realize what was possible for their own lives or their kids' lives. It was pretty powerful and made me feel like I had a greater purpose.

Turbo and I worked together for four months before I moved to a town about forty minutes away to start my master's degree. Even though I had physically put in a lot of effort, he was always right there alongside me, always willing to try. If something didn't work, we learned from it and built upon it. If something was a success, we wrote it down, recorded it, and bookmarked it. When we first met, he had said we would learn together, and that's exactly what we did.

It was rare for him to show emotion and be vulnerable, but in one of our last sessions, he gave me a hug and said, "What you've started is pretty special, kid. Don't stop now." He was right.

When I realized that the forty-minute drive might not be feasible to do three days a week, I reached out to Turbo for help in finding a new gym. He introduced me to Steve and Heidi Bowser, the owners of the CrossFit gym in my new town. They were gems. Both were supportive and enthusiastic about working with me, and I immediately took to them as well. Together, we decided that my journey as an athlete would continue, but it would remain in a private setting as I wasn't ready to be in a class yet. I was totally okay with this; I just knew I couldn't stop.

I was excited to share my "toolbox"—all the things that I had learned with Turbo—and to build on those successes. I had learned so much, but I knew we were just beginning to scratch the surface of my greatest potential as an athlete.

Much like Turbo, Heidi was patient and kind, and unafraid to try new things. I loved that she didn't treat me like a fragile doll. She treated me like an athlete. As my journey in CrossFit began to evolve, so did my following on social media. It happened organically, but to my surprise, it happened pretty quickly. At first, it was a couple of hundred people who I would interact with in the comments section or through my direct-message inbox, and at the time I thought that was a huge honor as well as a big responsibility. People were choosing to follow my page because they had seen something in my content that inspired them and motivated them to keep moving. I started to feel a sense of responsibility when hundreds of followers turned into thousands. I loved that my message and purpose were reaching so many, but now I couldn't stop. People were counting on me and, as a result, I felt like I needed to continue to challenge myself and them.

My initial reason for trying the sport of CrossFit was to become a better handcyclist, and I hadn't forgotten that goal, I went from completing a marathon in 4:34:16 to a year later completing that same race in 3:22:39. Whatever I was doing was working. I was stronger, faster, and had found a community of people who I felt understood me. I loved handcycling, but after a while, my heart began pulling me further in the direction of the CrossFit gym. It was challenging, but we experienced something new every day, and that's what excited me the most. I wasn't going to hang up my helmet for good, but I knew I had a lot more to offer the sport of CrossFit. I just needed to figure out what that would look like, and that was going to require a laser focus.

If I was able to become a CrossFit athlete, would I be able to become a coach?

As I increased my proficiency with movement and continued to understand that my body could endure a lot more than I thought it could, my curiosity about other adaptive athletes in this sport of CrossFit began to grow. My social media platforms became an amazing tool to connect with people all over the world. While I seemed to be the only woman with CP doing CrossFit at the time, I certainly wasn't the only adaptive athlete. At the end of 2012, I connected with Jason Strum and David "Chef" Wallach at CrossFit Rubicon in Tysons Corner, Virginia. Chef was the owner; Jason was the head coach. Jason was a single-leg amputee who had lost his leg at the age of twenty-two. He had joined the U.S. Army after high school and was taking part in a training exercise at Fort Drum in New York when there was an accidental explosion. The explosion killed two fellow soldiers and left Strum with a severely injured left leg. By the time we connected, he had been an amputee for several years. After seeing some of my training content, he became motivated to learn more about working with athletes with CP

He mentioned that if I was ever coming to town to let him know because he and Chef would love to meet me. As fate would have it, I had family in Maryland and was going to be visiting them for a week while I was off from school. It was winter break from my master's studies, the holidays were right around the corner, and I was spending the next few days with my aunt, uncle, and their three boys. Going to their house and being around them was like taking a vacation to Disney World. Their house was so full of love, and they had always been supportive of everything I had done in my life, but we didn't get to see each other as often as we would have liked.

It was about a forty-five-minute drive from Maryland to Tysons Corner, and I would need my uncle to drive me in the midst of the holiday chaos. But once I shared with my uncle why making this drive was so important to me, he didn't hesitate: he told me to start getting details so we could make the trip. I was really excited. This was an opportunity to finally meet people who not only understood what it meant to adapt the sport of CrossFit but who were immersed in the community and culture. CrossFit Rubicon was known for its community of adaptive athletes, mainly veterans, and I was so excited for what I might be able to learn just by being in the building.

As we drew closer to our destination, I started getting a little nervous. I had done my research and seen many pictures of the gym online. I felt as though I knew everything there was to know about this gym, but I wondered what it would be like in person. The real world is always different from digital representations, and sometimes not in a positive way.

It was late in the afternoon when we pulled into the parking lot. I could see the gym was full of people. We had arrived in the middle of a class. We parked in the front of the building but then realized the ramp access was in the back, so I decided to just take the stairs. It might have taken me twice as long to get into the gym, but with my uncle behind me, one crutch in my right hand and my left hand clutching tight to the railing, I made my way up the stairs. I felt victorious, and I hadn't even stepped into the building yet.

The front door was open, and as we stepped inside, the first thing that caught my eye was the "DEMAND MORE OF YOURSELF" mural on the back wall. I'd seen it in almost every picture online, so to see it in person felt surreal. Although the building was massive—a wall of whiteboards, fitness equipment, and people everywhere—at the same time, it felt inviting. As we watched twenty or so athletes finish their workouts, I was reminded of my first day at the Garage. Fist bumps, high-fives, and people on their backs trying to catch their breath but still smiling and looking like they had just accomplished something impressive. It was kind of like the universal sign of success in the sport of CrossFit.

Once the class had ended, Chef and Jason both noticed us, walked right over, and gave me a big hug. It was as if we'd known each other our entire lives. Their presence felt familiar, and at that moment, all my nervousness disappeared. I was just overwhelmed with excitement. We talked for about an hour or so while I showed Jason how I did certain movements like burpees, pull-ups, sit-ups, and even running on my crutches. It became clear that the one hour we had agreed to wasn't going to be enough for us to say and do everything we wanted to. It was getting late, so they invited me to come back and join their morning class the next day. When my uncle said he was willing to make the trip again, I got very excited. I'd never really been part of a group class before. I'd been so used to one-on-one sessions, I was a little apprehensive about how this would go, but they promised me I'd be in good hands with Jason coaching.

I left that day feeling so full of excitement and hope. This gym wasn't like anything I had ever seen. While my time with Turbo and Heidi had been an educational experience in the six months I had been doing CrossFit, this was the first time I felt like someone could truly understand what adaptive fitness felt like. I couldn't wait to go to bed because the next morning I was going to be back for my first group class.

The next day, back in the car, as we got closer to the gym, the nervousness started to creep up again. I knew

I'd be in good hands with Coach Jason, but would the other athletes care if I was in their class? Would they care if I was moving slower or doing something different? When we got to the gym, we climbed back up the steps, opened the door, and saw those same four words on the back wall: "DEMAND MORE OF YOURSELF." Yep, this was happening.

Before being called to gather at the whiteboard, I went to say hello to Chef. He gave me another welcoming hug and asked me how I was. "Excited!" I told him. From the corner of my eye, I could see Jason coaching an athlete before class started, and I turned to Chef and asked him, "So, do people really listen to him when he coaches?" It may have sounded a bit rude or strange, but that wasn't how it was intended. I had never seen anyone in the adaptive community be a coach, so to me, this was amazing. Chef laughed a little and said, "Hell yeah, they do! Jason is a badass coach." I never expected to say what I said next, nor expected to hear his surprising answer.

"Do you think people would listen to *me?* Do you think I could be a coach?"

"Not only do I think you can coach; you are going to work for me someday."

This conversation would change my whole life's trajectory; I just didn't know it yet. I smiled at him, said thank you, and then he told me to start making my way toward the whiteboard. We were about to begin, and I was going to be in my first mainstream class. When we got to the whiteboard, we were told that we would be paired with a partner. Not only was this my first mainstream class experience, but I was going to be doing my first partner workout. I was going to be paired with a complete stranger, and we were going to have to share the workout—nerve-racking but exciting. I would get to explain to somebody else how I would adapt our workout and, through the process, how we could share the workload equally and still have a great experience.

Jason went through the workout on the board. I found it easy to know what exercises I would need to adapt or change, so when it came time to pair up and go over the game plan, I felt confident about communicating it with my partner. Once we had our plan in place, it was time to complete the work.

That day, I fell in love with the concept of working in pairs. I loved having to share the work but also knowing that someone else depended on me to give my best effort. The high-intensity workout was a longer period (twenty-five to thirty minutes) than I was used to, and by the end of it, we were all high-fiving, fist-bumping, and breathing hard. No one cared how you adapted movements or if you had to scale certain things; everyone in that room was an athlete, and I knew then that I wanted to be part of this Rubicon community.

I left that day sweaty, tired, and full of gratitude. I was part of a new community, and though I wasn't sure when it would happen, I was already looking forward to an opportunity to return.

Once I was back in Davie, I shared my experience with Heidi. We talked about my mainstreaming into a few classes, and she was totally on board. I shared with her what Chef said about my coaching someday, and she said she would do anything she could do to help me pass the test necessary to become a CrossFit trainer. There was only one thing in the way: I was still enrolled in the master's program.

To graduate, I needed to complete a certain number of internship hours in the field that I wanted to specialize in. I came up with the idea to pitch a summer internship at CrossFit Rubicon to complete those hours. I went to the dean of my college and explained that my passion was in fitness and that I would be grateful to have her permission to complete my internship over the summer in Virginia. After a few discussions and explanations on how I could use my experience toward my overall degree, they gave me the okay to move forward with an out-of-state summer internship.

When Chef told me I'd be working for him one day, I never thought it would happen as quickly as it did. I left Rubicon in December and was back in April. I would be completing a full summer semester online as well as getting my training certification.

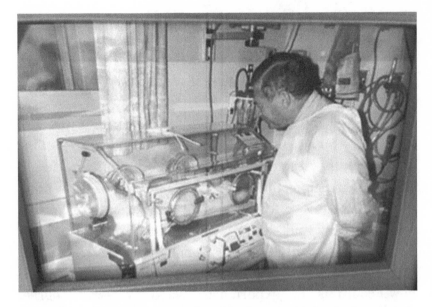

Grandpa admiring me at only a few hours old, in the incubator (1990)

Brandon and me at Viscardi (1993)

Grandpa bowling with me (1995)

The cover of Kids 'R' Us promoting the holiday children's coat drive (1995)

Toys "R" Us sales sheet (1996)

Toys "R" Us sales sheet for back-to-school (1996)

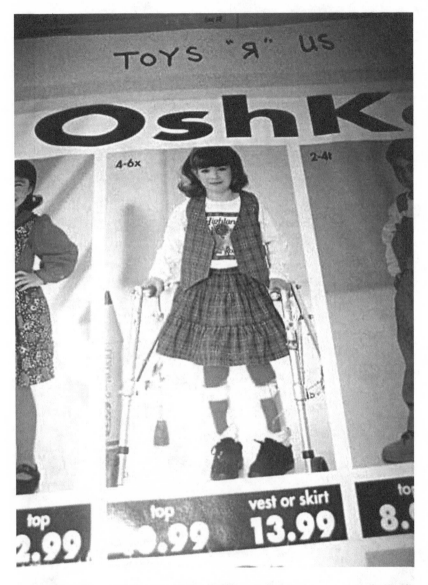

Modeling for the Toys "R" Us differently-abled toy guide (1996)

Modeling for Kids 'R' Us sales sheet (1996)

My first-grade class cheering me on at the empire state games
(1996)

Bubba and me on our way to Yankee Stadium (2005)

Me and date Steve prom night (2008)

Grandpa and me before prom (2008)

Grandma and me before prom 2008

Finish line of my first marathon (2011)

Me showcasing my abilities at Crush Games III (2013)

Crush Games 42lb Power Clean (2013)

Me showcasing my abilities at Wodapalooza (2014)

Me during a workout at CrossFit Conquest (2014)

Me on a track in Davie, FL during a Coach Hinshaw session
(2015)

Completing a workout with Brandon Fulwider by my side as my judge at Wodapalooza (2015)

Ty and Me in New York, right before my chemotherapy (Heidi Green photography-2016)

Me as a speaker at American College Personnel Association (2016)

Snapchat of me completing that work out at Wodapalooza
(2018)

Me training an athlete at Hammer Driven Fitness (2018)

Ty and me at the opening of Hammer Driven Fitness (2018)

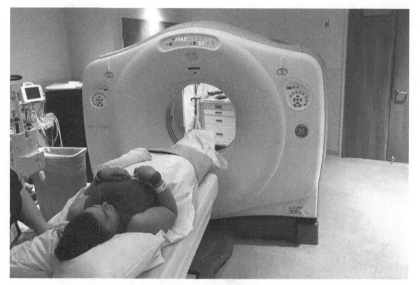

PET scan (2018)

Ty and me having a fun photoshoot done before starting
chemo (photo by Heidi Green 2016)

Family Photo: Me, Ty, and Hexi (EMOM Photography 2021)

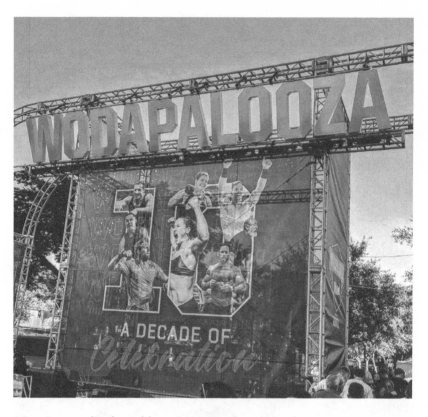

My picture displayed honoring Wodapalooza's ten-year anniversary (2022)

OUR STORY

Staying Driven is a live, interactive, online based experience. Fitness with *you* in mind!

Our vision is to create an affordable avenue that allows individuals to enjoy fitness from the comfort of their own homes. Our program is unique in the way we choose to cater to the specific needs of the adaptive and aging population. Our program merges top notch coaching with a supportive community to help everyday people achieve a greater fitness potential. This educational, interactive experience is available to the public regardless of age, location, abilities, or skill level.

Our mission is to educate, empower, and motivate athletes through fitness; giving everyday people the opportunity to celebrate success.

We look forward to seeing *you* at the virtual white board!

YOUR COACHES

Coach Steph   Coach Kelli   Coach Jordy   Coach Angie

Coach Brad   Coach Paul   Coach Bobby   Coach Bill

Staying Driven Coaching Staff (2022)

ONE FOR THE HISTORY BOOKS

The summer of 2013 was one for the history books—literally. After spending months interning at CrossFit Rubicon, studying the sport of functional fitness, and learning from so many, it was time for me to take my Level-1 training course. The CrossFit training certification course costs $1,000 and is presented over a two-day period. Participants are expected to retain a lot of information as well as go through a hands-on experience, simulating what it would be like to run a class in a CrossFit gym. And this was something that no woman with CP, to my knowledge, had ever accomplished before me.

I had become so involved in the community and so passionate about the people I was helping and those I might potentially help in the future that signing up for this certification was a no-brainer. It was definitely a financial investment as well as a time commitment, and I knew it was going to be a challenge, but other than that, it was an easy decision. I had signed up for the course a few months prior so that I could study the material as much as possible. Once you sign up for the course, become a registered participant, and your payment goes through, you are emailed a two-hundred-plus-page document that helps guide you through study materials. It was extremely overwhelming, but I knew that I had a lot of support in my corner, and I would do everything I could to pass this test. I was *driven.*

In CrossFit, they use the term "box" to describe the gym facility. I'd never been so nervous about entering a box before. I think I had put so much pressure on myself to not only pass the test but to be a woman who made history that I don't think I was truly present in the moment. Adding to my stress was that no one there looked like me; meeting the physical demands of the test was going to be daunting.

If I passed this course, I would be a CrossFit Level 1 certified trainer. I knew that I knew the information deep down, but I was doubtful I would be able to recall it all through my nervousness. I did pretty well on the practical portion, but the thirty multiple-choice questions on the test got the best of me. I had a feeling deep in my gut that I had failed the written test. We had to wait a week to find out our results—probably one of the longest weeks of my life. I would constantly check my email. Even though I knew they were pretty strict about the seven-day timeline, I felt that checking my email day after day would somehow make it appear faster. That was definitely not the case, and when I opened the email that finally arrived on the seventh day and saw "TEST RESULTS: FAILED," my heart immediately dropped into my stomach and I began to cry.

I was devastated. I badly wanted this. But looking back on it now, I'm grateful things happened the way they did. A few days later, I found out that I would have an opportunity to take the test again in just three weeks. I was excited and appreciative but also so scared. I didn't want this to be another wasted opportunity. I sat with Chef, the owner of CrossFit Rubicon, and talked about how I was feeling. He told me that I had an extreme amount of potential but that I was missing my own style. He then introduced me to his good friend Andrea. She was a successful CrossFit gym owner and coach, and although she was only about five feet tall, this beautiful woman presented herself with so much confidence and poise that meeting her for the first time was a bit intimidating. Chef had a strong sense that Andrea and I would be able to connect and work well with one another. As it turned out, he was right. Andrea was eager to help me and, more than anything, she wanted to see me succeed.

I knew a lot of things from the *CrossFit Training Guide* that was provided to me when I signed up for the course, but what she taught me, very quickly, was that it was okay for a trainer to have a unique style and not just live by the Guide. While making sure an athlete is moving safely and correctly is extremely important, nothing in the Guide indicated that having your own unique coaching style was a bad thing. I learned so much from working with both Chef and Andrea that, class after class, I became more confident. I loved gathering athletes around the whiteboard to explain the workout of the day and, with each class, I felt as though I was finding my style. I was able to command a room while making the athletes feel like they were being encouraged and motivated to be their best.

I spent about another six weeks studying and refining my skills before attempting the test again. I knew that I wasn't striving for perfection, but I was going to do everything in my power to pass this time around. Every new coach has an "aha" moment, a time when the knowledge, skill set, and practice come together and things just start to click. For me, that moment came while teaching an athlete how to do a "double-under" for the first time. A double-under is a movement often used in CrossFit programming; an athlete is jumping rope but moving fast enough and jumping high enough for the rope to pass under their feet twice before landing back on their feet. Being able to successfully coach this movement was a huge confidence builder. Jumping rope is a movement that I will never physically be able to perform, but the fact that I was able to successfully get the athlete to complete the task with verbal instruction was a pretty amazing feat.

When retake day arrived, I rolled in, crutches in hand, feeling so much more confident. I knew the retest did not require sitting through the entire weekend again, so that was a relief. When I took my seat in the box for the written portion, I was given a pencil, the test, and a Scantron. "You are allowed to begin. Best of luck," the moderator announced. As those words left the test moderator's mouth, my heart began to race. *What if I take this test and I fail again?!* Before my test anxiety could truly settle in and possibly sabotage my goals, I took a couple of deep breaths and reminded myself, *You know this information. You have been working so hard over the last couple of weeks to pass this test, and nothing is getting in your way.*

I didn't rush through the exam. I used all of the time allotted and made sure that I went over every answer. I felt confident afterward. It would still be a long seven days until I received my results, but I knew that I gave it everything I had, and I could only hope for a different result in return.

A week later, I frantically checked my inbox and quite possibly refreshed the screen more than two hundred times. The moment I saw an email come through from the CrossFit training department, I knew I was one click away from finding out the fate of my aspirations. I took a deep breath, clicked on the email, and quickly closed my eyes. I was frightened that I would see the same result as I had just three weeks earlier. Finally, I opened my eyes and saw the words: "CONGRATULATIONS, TEST RESULT: PASSED."

I couldn't believe what I was reading. I actually did it! I reread the email over and over, maybe a thousand times. Happy tears streamed down my face. I had made history by becoming the world's first female with cerebral palsy to successfully pass and obtain a CrossFit Level 1 training certification.

I was so excited to go into the box the next day and share the news with Chef, Andrea, and the rest of the Rubicon crew. I had done it! I had just gotten some amazing news that gave me the confidence I needed to continue to learn and grow as a coach.

I remember sensing something in my life had just shifted. Doors were about to open for me that would lead me to live one of my dreams. I couldn't play basketball and I couldn't create opportunities for adaptive basketball players, but I could make a difference by helping other adaptive CrossFit athletes. And, I thought, that's exactly what I am going to do. And then it hit me. The real source of my pride and accomplishment: I was about to keep my dear friend Scotty's legacy alive.

At the time, I had a small but steady following on Facebook and Instagram, but when I shared my historic accomplishment with them, I got an unexpected amount of support and excited reaction from almost everyone. Several of my followers spread the news to their social pages, and even more people began to take notice.

A few days after my initial post, I was contacted by somebody at CNN. They told me that Dr. Sanjay Gupta, CNN's chief medical correspondent, wanted to feature my story on a segment that they highlight as "the good stuff." I was so honored to be asked to do this interview. I was being given the opportunity to not only share my story but to shed some light on athletes like me. And I was going to be able to speak directly to these athletes and show them that they had potential and possibilities they might never have imagined. Thanks to people like Chef, Jason, and Andrea, this was becoming a reality.

The segment aired a day or two after I did the interview with Dr. Gupta. At that time, CNN news anchor Chris Cuomo was covering "the good stuff," and during his presentation, he referred to me as "the definition of good stuff." It was pretty surreal because people from all over the world were now introduced to who I was. What that meant to me was that adaptive athletes all over the world were now being introduced to their own potential.

You may remember me telling you about my first appearance on CNN. When I was seven years old, I was interviewed by a news anchor about Wheelchair Becky: Barbie's friend in a wheelchair. The title under my name read: "Stephanie Hammerman: Disabled seven-year-old." It was a great experience to be able to share Wheelchair Becky with the world, but it was also really nice to know that sixteen years later, I was able to put my stamp on a bigger accomplishment that wasn't defined strictly by my disability.

Shortly after the Dr. Gupta interview aired, my social media platform began reaching not just hundreds but thousands of people. Then I began getting phone calls, texts, and direct messages of support from people telling me how amazing it was to be sitting in a doctor's office or an airport and see my face on national TV. I would get a lot of messages from people living with cerebral palsy as well as parents of children with CP who would tell me that I was giving them hope that they or their child could live an active and healthy life as I did.

A bit later, I started hearing from people from all over the world telling me how much I inspired them and how I gave them an example they didn't even know existed.

I don't think I truly grasped how much of an impact I was having on the CP community at the time. It was overwhelming but in the best way possible. I was just grateful to know that my life and hard work were being recognized, allowing me to be the positive role model I wanted to be. This one interview snowballed into multiple media opportunities, giving me the ability to share my story on a larger scale.

I felt a sense of obligation to make sure that I was putting my best foot forward and leading by example. I began by documenting everything I was going through, even my personal struggles.

As my amazing summer and my time at Rubicon ended, I felt as though I was leaving my safe haven and my second home. My summer at CrossFit Rubicon truly changed my life. It changed the way that I viewed myself and the things that I was capable of accomplishing. And it helped me to understand that I could make a positive impact on others; I just had to follow my heart. I will forever be grateful for the guidance I received, the connections I made, and the confidence that was built in the summer I was there. The whole experience taught me that stepping out of your comfort zone can lead to some of the most amazing memories and experiences of your life.

It became apparent to me after that summer that I no longer wanted to pursue higher education. I wanted to be engulfed in fitness. But I had already come so far in the master's program that there was no turning back. Still, I sensed that with my newfound confidence and the growing audience I had access to, I was going to do something big. I decided that my best course of action was to get as involved in fitness at the university as I could.

No one with a physical disability had ever been hired to work at Nova Southeastern University's campus recreation facility, the RECPLEX. To me, this meant it was a challenge I had to take on. I knew that I loved working with and around fitness, and I knew that I was really good at interacting with people, so I applied for a front desk position at the university's 110,000-square-foot facility.

Securing the position did not come easy because administration officials believed I would not be able to handle the physical tasks that would be asked of me. All I needed was one shot, one opportunity, to prove them wrong. I got that opportunity thanks to a woman named Marcela, my direct supervisor at the RECPLEX. After a few conversations, she made it clear that she believed I would be able to do the job and that she saw a lot of potential in me. She was able to convince her bosses to at least give me a shot at proving myself.

Prove myself I did. In the year and a half that I worked there, I did everything I could to show that I was capable of handling all that the job had to offer. At first, I even took five a.m. opening shifts and was willing to do anything to impress on my bosses that anyone could hold the position of front desk supervisor. The job taught me a lot about the way people perceive individuals who live with different abilities, especially those of us who have to use accessibility devices to get around. People often make wrong assumptions, and the one thing that I loved most about working at the front desk and then working my way up to becoming a supervisor was that every day was an opportunity to educate and challenge the perceptions of what individuals with different abilities are capable of.

Front desk employees wore dark blue shirts, and front desk supervisors wore white shirts. The day I was able to put on my first white shirt made me extremely proud. I had worked very hard and had finally proven, not only to my supervisor but to her supervisor as well, that anything was possible and that making small accommodations so that employees with different abilities can be successful isn't anything to shy away from.

I loved my time working at the campus recreation center. Not only did it solidify the fact that my passion was really driven toward the fitness industry, but it taught me a great lesson: Continuing to be my own advocate is a pathway toward creating more opportunities for others.

THE WORST THEY CAN SAY IS 'NO'

I etched my name in the history books by becoming the world's first female with CP to become a CrossFit Level 1 trainer. I was heading back to South Florida with so much more confidence and the desire to expand on everything I had learned and experienced.

As soon as I moved back to Davie, I knew I wanted to find a new gym where I could coach. I dropped into a few boxes just to get the feel of the community, and one of the places I truly enjoyed was CrossFit Conquest. It was owned by two buddies, Johnny and Donivan. They were both very kind and welcoming, all while being able to command a room in a truly impressive manner. They were running big classes (ten to twenty). Athletes would gather in front of the whiteboard to discuss the upcoming workout, and the way the coaches were able to demonstrate movements, cater to athletes' needs, and safely coach everyone was like an art form. I spent the first few weeks there strictly as an athlete. They'd never had an adaptive athlete as part of their community, so this was a great opportunity to see how I would be received if I were to stay at this gym. It didn't take long for me to feel completely at home. One thing I love about the CrossFit community is how accepting everyone is. People would offer to help me set up or break down equipment when I needed it, and when they offered help and I declined, I was never questioned.

Johnny and Donivan were the first to give me an opportunity to work as a coach. They had a staff full of veteran coaches who had their own styles and athletes who truly respected them, so I'd be lying if I said I wasn't intimidated. The first few months I coached, it was like watching Bambi trying to stand for the first time. I would make silly mistakes and feel like I was crashing and burning, but everyone was extremely understanding. I wanted so badly to be a "good" coach that I was forgetting to find my own voice, my own style. Once I found my groove and truly understood the culture of Conquest, it was like something clicked and I was able to bring a new perspective while confidently embracing my ability to coach athletes on movements that I will never physically be able to do on my own.

I was at Conquest six days a week. If I wasn't coaching, I was training, and I loved every second of seeing how strong I had become. After workouts, people would just stick around and chat, and one afternoon, a few were talking about how they were planning to take part in a local competition called the Crush Games III. It was going to be happening at the end of the summer, and they were really excited about it. I have no idea what made me ask this question, but I asked if anyone knew who was running the event. Donivan said he knew him and was willing to make an introduction.

I knew I couldn't really "compete," but what if I could

use this opportunity to showcase what I was able to do for the local community? The worst thing the host could say was "no." Donivan gave me his contact and within a few hours, I got an answer. His name was Mike Osuna. He was a local fireman who also ran eight different CrossFit boxes in South Florida. He had been running this event for a few years but never had an adaptive athlete interested before, so this was new territory for both of us. I told him what I wanted to do. I didn't care what heats he put me in or what scores I received; I just wanted to showcase my abilities on the competition floor. I was hopeful that maybe I could inspire others to think differently. Mike immediately agreed. I was shocked. I was prepared for the answer to be "no;" I didn't quite think through the other option. But I was excited. I would be a very last-minute addition to the competition, so I was just grateful if I could do one workout—maybe two if I was lucky.

I soon learned that's not how Mike worked. If I was going to "compete," I was going to get the full experience of what it meant to be down on the competition floor. To do that, Mike assembled a small team to make sure I had everything I needed, from a lighter barbell to the weights I needed and even having Rogue Fitness build me a custom "rig" (a "squat rack") so I could feel comfortable completing movements like pull-ups and squats just like I would adapt them in the gym. Mike truly went above and beyond. He made sure I had everything when it came to equipment, but he also made sure I was assigned a one-on-one assistant for anything I would need before or during the event.

His name was Brandon. We had communicated via email a few weeks before the event, and he couldn't have been more accommodating. It was a bittersweet experience to meet and connect so easily with him. It brought up some of the sadness of my first love along with some of the joy. It took a bit of time before this Brandon became his own person to me and not a remembrance of someone else dear to me.

Mike asked me to meet with him and Brandon a few days before the event at the arena where the event was being held to ensure that all the details were discussed and any wrinkles ironed out before the event. Meeting them in person was exhilarating. A few months earlier, I had no idea this opportunity would have been possible, and now I was on my way to meet the team who were going to help me write my next story for the history books. I was nervous; I couldn't believe that this was actually happening. When I pulled up to the arena, Mike met me out by my car, directed me where to safely park, and then escorted me inside. It seemed like organized chaos. Rubber flooring was being placed, pull-up rigs were being erected, and volunteers were being pointed in various directions to bring this competition to life.

I'd never seen anything like it. As I was taking it all in, Mike introduced me to Brandon. He was going to be there for anything I needed as I navigated this experience. Brandon gave me a big hug and told me how excited he was to be working with me. Because we had been corresponding through email for a few weeks, he already had everything set up. Our main objective was to run through some of the movements and ensure I had everything I needed. Brandon was such a warm, encouraging, and kind soul. From the moment we met, it truly felt like a kinship, as if we had known each other our whole lives. He also wasn't a stranger to working with people with CP. He seemed at ease and talked to me just like he would anyone else. I would later find out that when he was a kid, he worked with a baseball team full of kids with CP. I trusted him immediately.

We spent about an hour going over everything I would need, how I would adapt the workouts, and the "game plan" I would follow to make the event a success. Five short workouts, five different opportunities to educate and engage the crowd just by doing something I had become passionate about. I left that night full of so much excitement and gratitude. I couldn't believe I was about to be a part of an actual CrossFit competition.

The morning of the competition arrived, and I could barely contain my excitement. I had no idea what to expect; all I knew was that I wanted to go out on the competition floor and make a statement. I got to the arena a little before seven a.m., met up with Brandon and Mike, and got ready for the first event. Being on the competition floor for the first time was an unbelievable feeling. The crowd was electric, and I could feel the love and support as I fought my way through the first workout.

I remember there being a lot of pull-ups. Brandon and I had set a standard for what would count as a "good rep," and if I didn't meet that standard, he would smile and say, "No rep." I remember feeling so relieved getting through that first workout. Once it was over, so many people were coming up to me telling me how impressed they were with what they had just witnessed and that I had truly inspired them with my presence on the competition floor. It was a wonderful feeling knowing that I had successfully done what I had intended to do, but the experience was far from over.

There were five different workouts, but the one I was most looking forward to was the "max lift: power clean". A power clean is a well-known powerlifting movement. An able-bodied athlete takes a barbell from the floor and finishes with the barbell on their shoulders. For me at the time, all of my power lifting/barbell movements were performed on my knees. It was the position that felt most comfortable and balanced.

The most I had ever been able to power clean was thirty-five pounds, and because of my CP, it took a little longer for my brain and my body to fully communicate with one another. Where most athletes would be "warming up" with some light weights, maybe some stretching, I was in the back explaining to Brandon that I needed to prepare myself by warming up with my heaviest weight. I got a few practice reps in and was feeling great. Brandon and I had a game plan. I was going to make the most of the time on the clock and try to hit a PR (personal record) of forty pounds. It was an aggressive goal, but when I looked at Brandon before going out on the floor, it was as if we both understood that I had every intention of smashing this goal.

We got out onto the floor, I met my judge, Brandon, and I showed her my standards of what good reps looked like. Then, I got set up. They had laid out a mat so I wouldn't damage my knees, so I found the spot that felt most comfortable on the mat, dropped to my knees, let go of my crutches, and pulled myself to an upright position to be able to start the movement. I heard the announcer's countdown: "Three, two, one...*go!*" And just like that, the clock started. In my first two lifts, I had twenty pounds on the bar, and it went up like butter. The bar was light, the music was blasting, and the crowd was full of energy. I told Brandon I wanted to up the weight by ten pounds. He did that, and I confidently raised the bar. The rep counted. The adrenaline was pumping, but the reality of the heavier weights coming up started to set in. Seven minutes had passed. I had successfully gotten up to thirty-five pounds and, with one minute left, Brandon looked at me and said, "Let's fucking go! You can do this. Trust me!" I looked at him, shook my head, and he loaded more weight onto the bar. I had about forty-five seconds to complete the lift, and on my first attempt at this new weight, I failed. I dropped the bar. Out of nowhere, the announcer looked at me and said, "Steph 'The Hammer' Hammerman in lane number twelve: She's got ten seconds... Can she do it?!" I popped the bar up with my hips and pulled my elbows through as fast as I could to get that barbell to my shoulders. I completed the lift with three seconds to spare. "Steph 'The Hammer' with a max power clean of forty-two pounds!" *Wait, what did he just say?! 42 pounds?!* I looked at Brandon, and all he did was smile and said, "I told you that you could fucking do it!"

That weekend changed my life. It wasn't long after that that people started recognizing me as Steph "The Hammer." After such a successful experience, I wanted to see what else was possible. I remember saying goodbye and thanking the whole team for what they had done for me. Brandon walked me out to my car and told that this wasn't going to be the last time I'd be doing something like this and that I had the power to change the world and do big things for this sport. Everything he said that day has come true, and I'm glad that almost ten years later, he's one of my biggest cheerleaders and greatest friends.

It wasn't long after the Crush Games that Donivan came to me and told me how amazing the experience of watching me was and that I should see if I could do something similar at this next event he was doing in January called Wodapalooza. By the end of the Crush Games weekend, I was definitely starting to drink the competition Kool-Aid, and if this was another opportunity for me to get in front of people and showcase what I had been able to do in the sport of fitness, I was all about it. I did some research and connected with the event organizer. His name was Guido Trinidad. He is the owner of Peak 360 CrossFit, and his event was to take place at Bayfront Park in Miami. I spoke to him only a few weeks after the Crush Games, and it didn't take long for him to agree to have me participate as an athlete at his event. Similar to the Crush Games, I informed him of all of my adaptations and a list of the equipment I would need. In exchange, he created a small team of people who would help me navigate the event. This was slightly bigger. It was a three-day event, giving me about eight different opportunities to be out in front of a crowd. The Miami experience was different mainly because people now knew who I was, all the workouts took place outside, and I had five more months of experience, so I felt a lot more confident.

The nickname "The Hammer" just stuck, so I embraced it. I had changed all my social media handles and even had a few news stories written about my experience competing over the summer, so being down in Miami felt like a completely different experience. Guido couldn't have been nicer. People often ask me how I got to do any of this, and the truth is that I just asked. I was the first adaptive athlete to ever showcase their abilities at a mainstream event, so even though this was a solo mission, it helped knock down some walls and opened doors for others in the years to follow. Wodapalooza was electric.

The crowds were so supportive, the fellow competitors were interested, and the organizers truly appreciated what I was bringing to the table. At the end of the three-day event, something very unexpected happened. I was invited to the awards ceremony. I knew I couldn't have landed on a podium, but I wanted to support the people who did and show my appreciation. To my surprise, one of the last awards given out was the "Spirit of the Games" award. Guido got up on stage and began to praise my efforts and what I had done to enhance the

2014 competition experience. He gave a beautiful speech and then awarded me with a trophy, a handwritten letter, and a swag bag. To me, the weekend was a success, but it was just the beginning.

A few days later, when all the excitement had settled, I met Guido and his planning team at his gym. I wanted to be involved, but I wanted to see how they would feel about trying to expand the adaptive experience. To my knowledge, no mainstream competition had ever hosted an adaptive division, so during this meeting of the minds, I asked if they would be willing to add an adaptive division. Without an ounce of hesitation, Guido excitedly said, "Yes!" In January 2015, Wodapalooza proudly hosted the first-ever adaptive division in a mainstream event.

Some people have referred to me as the godmother of the adaptive CrossFit world, but to me, I just saw a void and knew something could be done to fill it. I was born with a big mouth and a pretty face for a reason. I have always been one to speak up and blaze my own trail. This was no different. When I started getting deeply involved in the adaptive CrossFit world, I started to think back to the last conversation I had with Scotty before he died. I knew I wasn't going to be able to hop in a power chair and change the wheelchair basketball world, but what if I could celebrate his legacy in a new way? Like creating more doors of opportunity for adaptive athletes in the sport of CrossFit.

One question. One "yes." It all led to a life full of passion I never knew was even an option. I guess that's what happens when you are constantly reminding yourself that failure is not an option. Thanks to people like Mike, Brandon, and Guido, one simple "yes" turned into history-making action. Use this as your reminder: If you want something bad enough, go after it. The worst anyone can say is "no," but be sure to be prepared for a "yes" because it could completely change your life.

SWIPED RIGHT INTO FOREVER

On Halloween night in 2015, I was twenty-five, living in Davie, Florida, single, and not dating anyone. So, when my roommates headed out with their significant others and suggested I join them, I appreciated the offer but didn't really feel like

going out. Number one, I am *not* a fan of that holiday, and number two, I didn't feel like third-wheeling it, so I stayed in and watched some TV. I can't remember the show, but it was probably something truly enlightening like *The Real Housewives* or something on MTV. A few weeks before this, I had been dumped by a guy I was seeing mainly because, as he said, "I don't have the time." I completely understood. He was a heart surgeon, and oftentimes our "dates" would happen when he got off a shift and I'd try my best to stay awake while he told me about his day. He was kind and very intellectual, but it was not a good match and we both knew that.

Ending that was difficult because, even though I knew it was right, I still had that little voice in the back of my head telling me how hard it was going to be to find *my* person. I was an attractive young woman who was a wheelchair user living with cerebral palsy. Plus, I was navigating around the term "chair chasers," a very real thing. I encountered a handful of guys who only wanted to get to know me because I used a wheelchair. Their interest was in the prospect of sleeping with me and somehow checking that off some bucket list of theirs. Well, the joke was on them because, while there were definitely some situations that were uncomfortable, I was proud of the fact that in my twenties, I knew what I was worth and what I deserved when it came to finding a man. I had decided in my teenage years that I was going to save my virginity and share that experience with someone who genuinely and unconditionally loved me.

I'm not sure people understand exactly what they're saying when they think they're saying something nice or giving a complement. But one of the most common things I would hear is, "You're so beautiful for a girl who uses a wheelchair." Trying to date while not being defined by the accessibility devices I used to live an independent life was definitely trying at times, but being a hopeless romantic, I knew I couldn't give up.

A commercial came on the television, and I decided to fire up the good ole Tinder app. For those who don't know, Tinder is a dating app that allows users to swipe on their phones to determine whether they want to connect with you based on what they see in front of them. Swipe right for yes or swipe left and move on to the next person. I honestly hated this app because it was hard to truly get to know someone based on a short catchphrase or bio and a few pictures of that person's best days. But I was bored, and it had worked to meet the heart surgeon, so why not try one more time? I have never been one to give up, especially when things seem tough. I couldn't let my love life be any different. For years, I had heard things like *there's someone out there for everyone* or *don't worry, maybe you'll find a handsome boy with CP—that would be good.* I used that as motivation. I was going to find my person. I had no idea how or when, but I didn't want to check anyone else's boxes when it came to my life. I was going to find love, and it was going to be unconditionally mine.

I had been swiping for about twenty minutes matching some guys and having conversations with them that were either extremely superficial or boring...or both. I remember that I would mention having CP and having one guy respond, "Yeah, I don't think I could do that. I'm just being honest." The truth is that every time I shared my CP with a guy and got a similar response, I wondered if I would ever find someone who could just take me for me.

It was around 8:30 p.m., and I was about to close the app and delete it from my phone when I decided to swipe one last time. His name was Tyler. He was thirty-two and lived in Plantation, Florida, which I would later find out was about six minutes from my house. He had the most amazing smile. I noticed that first. As I continued to examine his profile and read his bio, I learned he was a firefighter. That made me a little wary because I had dated a firefighter for a while and later found out he had a whole separate life I had no idea about. But something about this profile made me want to give him a shot. He had posted four to five pictures of himself, and as I swiped through them, I could sense he was genuine. There were no flashy pictures, none of him shirtless, and none that scared me. While his profile didn't include a novel describing his hopes and dreams for the future, I did find myself drawn to his pictures. In one, he was in a fire engine with a big smile on his face. In another, he was playing ice hockey, and in the last few photos, you could see he had a sense of humor because it was a collage of four different photos—the different stages of what it looked like as he cut his long locks and shaved his head. I thought they were so silly, and they made me laugh. I wondered why someone would post something like that on a dating site. At the same time, I enjoyed that he didn't take himself too seriously. (I would later find out that he donated his long hair to an organization that makes wigs for cancer patients.) I swiped right.

A few moments later, my phone lit up with a Tinder notification: "You and Tyler have matched." As I read those words, I got excited and then immediately overwhelmed with doubt. *Don't screw this up. Don't tell him right away.* I can't remember who messaged who first, but I do remember feeling a sense of calm wash over me as we got deeper into the conversation. Tyler was kind from his first message. He wanted to really know about *me*. I remember being so nervous about sharing who I truly was, but I had no choice. A few years earlier in 2013, CNN had aired a segment about my being the world's first female CrossFit trainer living with CP. After that, information about me was pretty easy to access. You could Google my name and find pictures of me on my crutches, using a chair, and engaging in fitness activities. I couldn't hide who I was anymore, so after a few minutes, I shared the following: "Before we get too deep into this, I need to know, would it bother you if I used a wheelchair and crutches? I have cerebral palsy." Tyler's response: "Would it bother you that I'm pigeon-toed?" I couldn't believe what I was reading! Did this guy just make a joke while looking past my differences? This was a game-changer.

We messaged through the app for about ten minutes before I took a leap and gave him my number. It was very clear that he was someone I wanted to continue to talk to. *Man, this guy was so easy to talk to! There's no way he could be real.* We texted the whole rest of his shift. He told me his fire station had created a haunted house for the neighborhood kids, and he was spending his shift passing out some candy and trying to make the most of being at work during one of his favorite holidays. When he got off shift, he told me he would be headed to his shop to work on some art. It was probably midnight by then, but we kept the conversation going. We had switched from texting to talking on the phone, and I remember thinking how handsome he sounded. I know that may sound ridiculous, but I now had a voice to add to the smile I saw in the pictures; I couldn't help but get excited. We talked for hours. I had to be up at four a.m., and by the time we said goodnight, it was around two a.m. I didn't get much sleep at all, but I woke up with the biggest smile on my face the next morning.

Would I hear from him again? I hoped so, but I had

left the ball in his court. I was honest with Tyler when I told him that I came with a few extra accessories, and he never once hinted that he was ready to run. This was a welcomed change, and if I never heard from him again, at least I knew there were men out there who looked deeper into a person than just focusing on what is seen on the outside.

I didn't have to wait long to find out if I would hear from him again. Before we had ended our phone call that night, or rather, earlier that morning, I had told Ty that I had to teach classes starting at 5:30 a.m. Wouldn't you know it, at 6:30 a.m., my phone lit up: *"Text From Tyler Tinder"* (yeah, I didn't know his last name). Receiving this text was a simple affirmation. I didn't dream it or make him up in my head. I had found a guy who was genuinely interested in getting to know me for me. We talked, texted, and even FaceTimed for a solid two weeks because I was a little apprehensive. I did, after all, meet this guy on a free dating app. On the other hand, he didn't just want to hook up. He wanted to genuinely form a connection. Call me crazy, but it was hard for me to believe. I knew I would be traveling for my good friends Angel and Jackie's wedding the next weekend, but we agreed that when I came back, and if things still felt right between us, we would go on our first date.

I was excited about the wedding festivities, and Ty encouraged me to enjoy the weekend and be present. I had been friends with Angel and Jackie for a few years, and watching their story unfold gave me a lot of hope. Angel had gotten a virus from surfing while on a vacation. The virus left him paralyzed from the waist down and having to use a wheelchair daily. His wife Jackie is able-bodied. Angel is an attractive man and his wife is gorgeous, so to me, this made total sense. But to the outside world, it's not always that easy to accept. Their relationship helped me to understand that a successful, loving partnership with someone who could look past an accessibility device was possible, and that gave me hope.

The wedding venue was reminiscent of a collage on a Pinterest board. The ceremony took place outside a beautiful old barn. Rows of white chairs were set up with a very long aisle for the bridal couple to walk down. The seating arrangement had been carefully planned to be as inclusive as possible with each row missing a few chairs to accommodate wheelchair users. And every seat was positioned to give every occupant a great view of the bride and groom. One of the details I noticed right away was a brown, wooden chair placed directly across from Angel. At the start of the ceremony, you could see Angel sitting up, staring at that empty chair as he anxiously awaited his new bride. Jackie was a stunning bride as she walked down the aisle dressed in traditional white. Watching her take each step, smiling as she went, made it difficult for me not to wonder what that felt like. *Would this ever happen to me? Would I ever find someone who would love me the way Jackie and Angel love each other?* Jackie sat in the chair across from Angel, and as they exchanged vows, she was able to look directly into his eyes as they each said, "I do."

One of my favorite memories of this day was when our

friend Zack brought Jackie's and Angel's rings to the altar. Zack has lived since the age of two with no legs after having them amputated due to growth deformities. He is known for getting around on a skateboard and doing all sorts of crazy tricks with his wheelchair strapped to him. He is one of the strongest people I know and happens to have one of the biggest hearts and a bit of showmanship in him, so it was no surprise when he made a grand entrance as the ring bearer. The officiant asked for the rings, and all I heard was Zack screaming, "I'm coming, Jackie! Wait." And as he said that, he sped down the aisle on his skateboard, came to a screeching halt, and handed over the rings. It got a huge laugh, and I don't think Jackie and Angel would have wanted it any other way. The ceremony came to a close as they shared their first husband and wife kiss, made their way back up the aisle, and with much excitement, let all of the guests know it was time to party!

The reception took place inside the beautiful, rustic barn. Round tables with chairs were set up all around the barn with a few spots left open at each table for those who brought their own chairs or wheelchairs. Each table had a dark-blue tablecloth, simple white flowers that protruded from what looked like a small tree stump in the center, and a few white candles. There were little white lights hung from the rafters that twinkled and swayed in the slight breeze blowing through the open barn doors. The setup was simple yet elegant. The room was filled with so much love. There were no assigned tables, so guests could sit wherever they chose. When I saw

Jackie for the first time after the ceremony, she hugged me, and I began to cry. I wasn't sad. I was inspired. I told her how beautiful she looked and that their love story gave me hope that one day, a day like this would happen for me too.

The party was so much fun. The music was great, and I was out on the dance floor with a bunch of old friends, without a care in the world. The energy in the room was electric, and that night will stay with me forever. Still, every time a slow song came on, I couldn't help but think about Tyler. I remember that I texted him during the reception and told him, "I wish you were here," and he responded, "Soon enough, enjoy the wedding." I guess weddings can make a person all dreamy-eyed. Or maybe I just needed the inspiration from this particular wedding. But I decided that day that when I got home, I was going on a date with Ty from Tinder.

My flight home was the next day. I arrived at the Houston airport early and had about an hour and a half to kill before my departure, so I texted Ty and asked him if he wanted to FaceTime. Hearing his voice and seeing his smile gave me butterflies. As cliché as that sounds, it was true, and I wasn't about to fight that feeling. I deserved this. I sat in that airport and FaceTimed for what seemed like five minutes when in reality we had been talking, laughing, and flirting with each other right up until it was time for me to board. Once I got settled into my seat, I texted him, asking how long I'd have to wait to see him. He asked me what I was doing the next night to which I simply answered, "Yes."

I had no idea where we would go on our first date or what to expect except that he hinted at dinner. When the date night came, all I knew was excitement; I really wanted to spend time with this guy. The only thing I shared was my laundry list of food allergies: peanuts, tree nuts, coconut, carrots, green beans, and grapes; I was game for anything else and hopeful he could find a place without too much trouble that wouldn't kill me.

Date night came on November 17, 2015. I decided to dress simply: dark jeans, a grey tank top, a gold, sparkly sweater, and a pair of my favorite Converse sneakers. This "simplicity" was actually a level up for me because I normally wear yoga pants and a tank top every day. I was very nervous and hopeful that this meeting would go well. We had just built a really nice connection over the phone, so I was optimistic that it would translate to real life.

Moments before I heard his knock at my door, all of these random thoughts started running through my head: *What if seeing me walk scares him away? What if he notices people staring at us? Will he care?* Then I remembered that he drove a pickup truck, and I became anxious about how he might handle having to help me navigate the big step up into the truck. *Would my reality freak him out?* I hoped he would be okay with helping me get in and all of my angst. I was a mess. I shook those ugly questions from my head and answered the door.

The minute it opened, I saw Ty's smiling face, and every bit of worry disappeared. There he was: Tyler from Tinder. Six-foot-three, dark hair, and the best smile I had seen in a long time. He was wearing a Johnny Cash graphic tee, jeans, and to my surprise, matching Converse shoes. We laughed, shared a big hug, and then headed to his truck. He had a dark-blue Dodge. I love trucks, but I still wondered how I would tackle getting into his truck without making a complete ass of myself. Before I could conjure up a plan, he asked me if I would mind if he just picked me up. I didn't, so he did. Honestly, it was like we had done this all the time. He was a fireman, so I knew he had experience in assisting and even carrying people, but to his credit, he didn't make it a thing. It took him all of about ten seconds: He placed me in the seat, helped me buckle up, got behind the wheel, and off we went.

During our drive, he told me we were going to the drive-in theater in Fort Lauderdale. He was taking me to see *The Peanuts Movie* because we had talked about how much I enjoy animated films. As I looked about the cabin of his truck, I saw a cooler placed neatly behind the driver's seat in the small space that separated the seats from the truck bed. He had taken the time to pack a little picnic cooler for us. On top of the cooler were a few tablets of Benadryl. I laughed when I saw them and he said, "I wasn't quite sure how bad your allergies were so, just to be safe." This guy listened. He didn't once make mention my CP, and he made an effort not to kill me on our first date. I would say it was already pretty romantic.

We got to the drive-in, purchased our tickets, and as we were trying to find a place to park, we got into a fender bender. No one was hurt, and he tried to play it off, but I knew he was a bit nervous. We laughed about it, made light of the situation, and then went back to enjoying each other's company. We talked through ninety percent of the movie. I remember just wanting to get closer to him, wanting to hold his hand, and every time I would see him smile, I wondered what it would be like to kiss him.

As the movie was nearing the end, I went after what I wanted. He had a bench seat in the truck, so I slid closer to him, told him I wanted to just relax with him, and that I was having the best time. He told me he was too. He helped me slide my feet up toward the door so my head was against his chest. We flirted back and forth and, after a few minutes, I told him he was being a tease because all I really wanted to do was kiss him. He smiled. We kissed. It was like we had been dating forever. It felt so natural and comforting but exciting all at the same time.

By the time we finished our kiss, the movie had ended. As the credits rolled, Ty asked me what I wanted to do next. By now, it was way past my bedtime, but I was awake and eager to spend as much time as possible with him. We decided on the beach.

The beach was about a five-minute drive from the drive-in. Ty parked as close as he could to the sand, and we hopped out of the truck and started walking to the beach. I had my crutches and, from many failed attempts at walking in sand, often finishing with me horizontal on the beach, I knew that this was going to be difficult to manage. I took a deep breath and tackled the situation like I would any other challenge—head-on. I struggled to stay upright while walking down toward the water, but I must have been successful at my attempts because Ty didn't seem to notice—or he pretended well.

It was dark, and a man following behind us was trying to remain patient despite our slow pace. Sensing the man's impatience and in no particular hurry of his own, Ty just aimed his flashlight at the guy and said, "Oh, no, you can just go ahead of us." He didn't try to make me hurry.

I couldn't believe how this night was ending. And I couldn't stop smiling. *Was I dreaming?* Ty asked me if I wanted to sit down with him. Sand and CP are unlikely friends, but we made it work. He sat directly behind me, wrapped his arms around me, and we continued our conversation without skipping a beat. As each wave crashed onto the shore, we got deeper into our conversation.

We talked about our families—mine large, his not. Ty's mom works for a home builder and has so many roles doing that. His dad's background is as a general contractor, but he has spent many years doing insurance investigations for law firms, specifically involving high-rise buildings. His dad learned how to play hockey at the age of forty-six in order to share in one of Ty's passions. Ty played hockey every Sunday as a goalie, which he'd been playing since he was six years old.

I learned that Ty's parents had a good relationship and had been together for more than thirty years, the complete opposite of my family experience. Ty said he still had a good relationship with his parents, which was refreshing to hear because my family drama was more than enough for one relationship. Then we talked briefly about religion. I shared my not-so-religious Jewish heritage with him, and he shared his Christian background with me.

Ty was baptized as a Methodist and attended a Methodist church for about ten years. After that, he attended a Lutheran private school. From his Lutheran teachings, he adopted the viewpoint of accepting others' religious beliefs along with gaining an understanding of the differences and the commonality among religious messaging. He is not of any particular religious bent and neither tries to force his religious beliefs or his relationship with God on others nor does he ask others to convince him of theirs. So, there we were and are, a sort of Jew with a sort of Christian who basically believe that if you're not hurting anyone, it's all good.

After our short examination of our religious standings, Ty lightened the conversation with a story about his first visit to New York City. He had pictures on his phone to go with the story, so it was a bit of a nice show-and-tell. He and his parents were traveling to Vermont for a family gathering, and Ty convinced his parents to take a side trip to NYC so they could take the Big Bus Tour—he argued that NYC was kind of on the way. But their flight from Philadelphia was delayed for three hours, and they got stuck in Philly. They reserved a hotel room for the night, and the next day, Ty booked them on Philadelphia's Big Bus Tour. Like NYC's, these tours are on double-decker buses. They provide a quick view of the city while a guide, often telling humorous anecdotes, informs you about the important things that happened in the city's history. Think of it as a living, humorous history cheat sheet. After that, they managed to still make a stop in NYC for a night and take—you guessed it—the Big Bus Tour. To this day, Ty quotes ridiculous "facts" from these two history lessons. And that is how the night went. Nothing to write about (yet I did), but so very important to me as a glimpse into how the two of us could be. We were *simpatico* in many ways.

Oh, I also learned that Tyler from Tinder had a last name: Roach. Tyler Roach. But all of his friends and the people closed to him called him Ty.

That night on the beach was the first time I ever pictured what it might look like to be deserving of true love. Ty was a man who was honest, kind, funny, intelligent, and unafraid of staring societal perceptions in the face. I can't say I believe in love at first sight, but what I can tell you is that this would be the beginning of learning what it means to be unconditionally loved.

NEW ADVERSITY, NEW ADVENTURE

I've spent the last eight years of my life focused on my health and creating a better future for myself. I found a passion for fitness, and I figured out how to make a career out of that passion. But what happens when, in one moment, all of that hard work doesn't seem to matter?

People tell me that I was born a fighter and that I've conquered cerebral palsy. While I understand where they are coming from, the truth is that I haven't conquered anything. I just learned to accept it and live my life with it to my greatest potential.

My life was changing in ways I could never have imagined but I had always hoped for. Earlier, I had found a job doing what I loved as a CrossFit trainer and settled into an apartment where I felt comfortable and could live independently. As the weeks and months went on, my training became more consistent. I was experiencing many firsts together with Ty, from meeting his family to our first getaway weekend together and finally taking our relationship to a deeper intimate level. He made me feel seen, confident, and sexier than I had ever felt before. I was falling in love. And I was doing what I treasured most as a job; everything in life seemed to finally be coming together. I felt as though I was on top of the world.

That feeling didn't last as long as I thought it would.

As a CrossFit trainer, working out was part of my daily routine, sometimes even twice a day. I knew something was off when my desire to work out and push myself became less consistent and my work schedule became grueling. I was not acting like myself. I had gotten so caught up in my own head that I started experiencing symptoms of depression. I cried more often than smiled and started highlighting negatives instead of focusing on all the good that was happening around me. And my relationship with Tyler began to suffer. I had a man who truly cared for me, yet I tried to push him away.

I had spent so many years not believing in my self-worth that when someone came around and tried to prove to me that I was worthy, I tried to self-sabotage. I started arguments for no reason and told Tyler I wasn't sure how I felt about him because it seemed easier. If he walked away, it would be something I knew how to cope with. As crazy as it may sound, having someone love me unconditionally was brand-new, scary territory.

Thank goodness he stuck with me during some of those tough days because he quickly helped me recognize that how I was acting was extremely out of character for me. As the weeks went by, I began to see that I needed to change my attitude toward many things in my life or else I was going to lose those who brought me happiness. That's when I decided I needed to go back to therapy and talk to a professional.

I should have known something still wasn't right when I was mentally feeling better but my physical drive for life was not returning. I no longer had the energy to work out every day, and my work schedule—waking up at four a.m. and closing the gym at nine p.m.—began to take a toll. To me, pushing myself to exhaustion was normal. *If you want to reap great rewards, you need to work harder than the next person.*

My first symptom that should have served as a warning was when Ty was holding me one night and then suddenly moved away from me for no apparent reason. I thought I had done something wrong, which upset me, and I questioned him. He told me it wasn't something I did. It was because I was sweating so profusely, he was actually getting wet from holding me. My body was giving me a signal.

The next symptom appeared after Ty and I had just come home from a nice dinner at our usual haunt, Panera Bread—we aren't fancy folks. I went to use the bathroom and when I began to transfer back into my chair, I felt this sudden, unbearable pain in my right armpit. At first, I thought it was a nasty bruise I might have gotten from a workout earlier that week, but as the pain began to radiate, I felt a golf-ball-sized lump in my armpit. I started to panic and called for Ty to come take a look. He had spent nine years as a firefighter paramedic, so as soon as he felt the lump, he knew something was wrong. He kept me calm but told me that we needed to make an appointment to see my doctor first thing on Monday morning.

That Monday, April 18, at eleven a.m., while Ty and I were sitting in the doctor's office, myriad scenarios ran through my head, none of them good. *What could this be?* That was the big question circling my brain. I was called to the doctor's exam room, and when she came in, I was hit with another round of angst. I thought I had made an appointment with my regular doctor, but as luck would have it, she had called out sick that day. So, there I was, facing an unknown illness with an unknown and, to me, untested doctor. Ty could tell I was starting to get nervous, so he did what he does best; he grabbed my hand and made me smile. The doctor felt the lump under my armpit, and then she moved up my body and found a few more of these lumps on both sides of my neck. *Are you serious? What are they?* The doctor saw the concern on my face, so she explained that these were enlarged lymph nodes. Now, I am probably one of the world's most emotional people, so as soon as I heard this, my tears began to flow. When something is deemed abnormal, my brain starts wandering and creating the worst of the worst-case scenarios. I immediately started running some of these scenarios through my head, none of which were good and all of which ended with the "big C." I was scared shitless and began to tremble with fear.

Ty is one of the most loving, compassionate people I know, but in times of chaos, he's very calm and rational. At that moment, I didn't want rational. I didn't want unwarranted panic to go along with mine either. I wanted to feel protected and safe and maybe a bit of sympathy.

The doctor left the room for a few minutes and came back with a script in her hand. "We are sending you to get an ultrasound of your neck and breasts next Wednesday morning," she said. "Swollen lymph nodes can be caused by many different things, but I want to be safe rather than sorry." *Swollen lymph nodes...breasts... My ugly scenarios were being given life.*

I took the script from the nurse with a surreal calmness and thanked her...and we left. Everything now began to move at lightning speed. I had planned to fly to Arizona to visit family that Wednesday night at six p.m., but now I had reservations. *Will all this testing be done by then? Will I be healthy enough to go on the trip?*

Wednesday's doctor visit came sooner than I thought it would. Ty and I pretty much sat in silence all the way to the office. I was "in my head" a majority of the time, but my hand was always in Ty's hand; I never felt like I was alone.

With my man by my side, I entered the examination room. It was a room with nothing on the walls except a small clock. The room was so quiet, I could hear the secondhand ticking. When the technician began administering the ultrasound, I tried to be stoic and find my positive place. Every so often, I would feel Ty's warm hand on my cold leg and a sense of calm would come over me. The entire process took about ninety minutes. I put my clothes back on, and we waited for the radiologist to come in and explain what they had found.

Thirty minutes later, a petite woman with a welcoming smile walked in. "Good morning, Steph," she said in a soft voice. "From what I can see, there's nothing to worry about in your breast tissue [this was part of the overall testing process], but we found a few spots on your neck and armpit that are questionable."

I was glad they had done a very thorough test, but honestly, it felt like we still had no answers. This was really hard for me, especially because we knew something wasn't right, but nobody could tell us what was going on. I felt as though these medical professionals might know something but were just too scared to tell me. I hated the feeling of my body trying to fight something I couldn't control.

Fortunately, my primary doctor was down the street, so as soon as we got the test results, we headed directly there. She told me she would need to take blood work and set up an appointment with a radiologist for me to get a biopsy. *Did she just say biopsy? Holy shit, do they think I could have the "big C?!"*

A little while later, the only words echoing in my head were "radiologist" and "biopsy." *Was this really happening to me? And what about my trip? Could I still go?* The answer to that question was yes. I would be gone for six days while doctor appointments would be scheduled for my return. I was allowed to go *enjoy* my trip—doctor's orders.

By this time, it was about 12:30 p.m., and my plane would be departing in just a few hours. I was an emotional mess. I didn't want to say goodbye to Ty, I didn't want to wait six days to start getting answers, and I sure as hell didn't want to sit on a plane for five hours with nothing to do except think about all that had happened in the last few hours. But I had no choice.

Normally when I'm in the airport, I take full advantage of my time rather than just sticking my head in my phone. I like to people watch and enjoy the different dynamics of their interactions. Often, I find someone to talk to, and I've even formed friendships while waiting for a flight. I always have business cards with me and find this time a good opportunity to network. But this time, I felt numb. As I made my way to the gate, all I could think about was the possibility of being very sick. *I hadn't been ill in years; was this some sick and twisted way to tell me I needed to take a break?*

It felt as though I was in the air for twenty minutes rather than five hours. I felt foggy. I needed to try my best to be present, but I was really scared. As the plane landed, I took a deep breath knowing I needed to get my shit together. I was going to be in Arizona for four days with my grandparents to celebrate Passover, and they didn't need to see me like this.

The first day with everyone was okay. I was tired, but it was nothing I couldn't handle. I played Rummikub and Pictionary, joked around with my siblings and cousins, and I ate a lot at the Seder meal. By the second day, I was hit again with the feeling that something wasn't right. I went to the local CrossFit gym and couldn't finish a workout that was programmed for me. My energy level was low, and I felt weak on my feet. The symptoms only got worse as my visit to Arizona progressed. *This can't be happening to me. I have so much to do.*

My trip wasn't over in Arizona. For months, I had been planning to head to Cookeville, Tennessee, home of the four-time CrossFit Games champion, Rich Froning Jr. Rich and I had worked out together a couple of years earlier and, though we both had worked with the same endurance coach, Chris Hinshaw, we had never trained together with Chris. Chris normally only coaches elite athletes, so it was a privilege to train with both of these well-known, accomplished athletes, and I was determined to make the best of it.

I landed in Nashville early Sunday morning, and although I wasn't feeling well, I was excited to be there. Chris had created a workout that both adaptive and elite athletes could complete together. The workouts were split into intervals and adjusted for the individual athletes' abilities but designed so that both athletes would complete each interval at the same time. Chris had a relationship with some folks at Reebok, and he thought they would be interested in seeing a video of this unique approach and how it integrated athletes with dynamically different backgrounds and abilities.

In the two days I was there, we got a lot accomplished including capturing video content of the workouts and taping interviews with the participants. We also formed new friendships. Still, I couldn't shake the nagging feeling that my tank was running on empty. Unfortunately, Reebok decided not to accept the project, so it never went any further. However, the experience for me was tremendous, and just being asked to be a part of the project was an affirmation that my dedication to my career was paying off.

The next night, I was going to head back home to Florida, but cold symptoms hit me like an eighteen-wheeler. I called my doctor and scheduled an appointment for the day I was to return. For the first time, alone in my hotel room, I cried. I thought of the real possibility that this could be cancer. Why else would they use words like biopsy, radiology, and ultrasound? I had allowed that thought to flash through my head before, but as the days passed and I got weaker, that fleeting thought became a constant companion. When Ty picked me up from the airport the next night, he could tell that something wasn't right. I assured him that I had made an appointment for the morning and that we would soon find a way to treat whatever was going on.

The next morning felt like déjà vu: Ty and I sitting in a doctor's office, waiting for them to call my name, and when they did, going back to the all too familiar exam room. This time, my symptoms were quite noticeable: congestion, coughing, sneezing, achiness, and fever. *This couldn't be cancer; this had to be some sort of cold or flu.*

When we arrived, Ty could tell I had gone from a bit worried to all-out scared. He reached over, kissed me, and said, "I'm right here, I'm not going anywhere." That sense of calm came over me again, and I mustered the courage to get out of the car. We sat in the waiting room for what seemed like an eternity (more like ten minutes), and when they called my name, my heart began beating fast. All I could think about was that my body was telling me that something was wrong, and I had a feeling that soon the doctors would echo that dread.

We made our way back to the examination room, where I was so relieved to see the doctor I trusted. Maybe she would say everyone else had missed the mark and I just had a cold. I looked at her, smiled, and hoped. Unfortunately, her answer wasn't that simple.

My doctor looked at me and spoke to me with compassion and empathy, but her opinion had not changed: I needed to have the biopsy done whether I wanted to or not. I left with a handful of decongestants and no good news.

On that Friday, April 29, at eleven a.m., Ty and I entered the building where this biopsy was going to take place. In my head, I pictured another bleak place with empty, off-white walls, but to my surprise, when we opened the door, it revealed a beautiful office This area of the building must have been renovated within the last year. The atmosphere seemed bright, and all the receptionists and nurses were welcoming and calming. I signed in and was almost immediately taken back to the room where the procedure was going to take place. As we entered the room, I couldn't help but marvel at how wide the doors in the facility were. It was so easy to maneuver in my wheelchair and such a different vibe from the last appointment.

The nurse came in to take some preliminary information, and then the doctor walked in a few minutes later. I immediately noticed how attractive he was. I know my boyfriend, who I love dearly, was in the room, but if I was about to get cut open, I can't say I was too upset that Dr. McDreamy (professionally known as Dr. Peter Swischuk) was going to do the job. Maybe I wasn't as sick as I thought?

The procedure seemed easier than I originally anticipated, but I don't know anyone who would enjoy having a needle the size of their arm injected into their neck. The doctor, learning that Ty was a paramedic and had a good amount of medical knowledge, invited him to watch the procedure. This ended up being a good thing because as I was hyperventilating from the realization of what was about to happen, Ty's presence helped to calm me. Unbeknownst to me, Dr. Swischuk had given Ty a cup to hold with a solution in it. He had told Ty that when the biopsy sample was removed, he would need to drop the sample into the solution. If it floated, that was a good sign; if it sank, it meant something was abnormal. Mine sank.

As soon as I recovered from the procedure and caught my breath, I heard Dr. McDreamy announce in a soft, seductive voice, "All done. I took out two really good samples. Everything went well, and I will see you in a week." Nothing was said to me about the sinking sample. What I did hear was "a week." *Why do all these tests take so long?*

On Friday, May 6, my phone rang. It was Dr. Swischuk's office. "We have your results, Ms. Hammerman," came the woman's voice on the other end. My heart sank. Something was wrong; I could feel it. "Can you come in this afternoon?" I told her we would be there as soon as we could. Since this horror began, Ty had not missed one appointment, and I loved him for it.

We got to the office around 11:30 a.m. after a very long week, and I was ready to get some answers. But I was also aware that those answers could be my worst-case scenario. I signed in, and they lead Ty and me right back to the same room where the biopsy was conducted a week earlier. I was hoping McDreamy would walk in and tell us I had nothing to worry about, but just like the first few doctor's visits, this hurdle was not going to be very simple to navigate. The doctor walked in and immediately handed me the pathology report.

"Well, we know something isn't right, but we don't exactly know what it is. You are going to have to schedule an appointment with a surgeon to get deeper inside the lump, and we are going to have to have them test the full sample," he stated, suddenly losing his dreaminess.

After a few minutes of trying to come to grips with having to go to yet another doctor, a surgeon, to have yet more of me removed for testing—and still having no concrete answers—I decided to take a different course. I called each of my parents separately to bring them up to date on what I had and hadn't learned from my tests. They both agreed that the best thing for me to do would be to come to New York and get the most advanced medical care available. So, almost before you could even say the words *New York City,* we were on the plane headed to stay with my mom (with my father still living just a town away) and eventually on to see the best doctors in the world. When I was eighteen, I vowed to never to live in New York again. I spent many years trying to shed that scared little girl that I once was and now that I had no other choice but to return, made this decision even more gut wrenching. Living in New York meant I would need to go into New York City from my mom's house on Long Island.

This trip would mark the first time that Ty and I traveled by plane together. That meant that Ty would have to learn how to navigate the airport and plane with someone with accessibility devices. That is a little bit more involved than you might imagine. When I arrive at an airport with my own powered wheelchair, I have to go through security like everyone else. But, unlike everyone else, I don't go through metal detectors. I am given the option of having a lengthy, public pat-down or being wheeled off to a private room. I always opt for the public option as I don't like the idea of being whisked away as though I have to be hidden from view. That is likely just a personal phobia or something, but that's me.

The pat-down is a lengthy process that involves security officials swabbing everything: my hands, feet, shoes, and chair. The whole process takes five to ten minutes. (Ty had to go through regular security and wait for me.) Once I am cleared, all of my carry-ons and my crutches have to go through a security check as well.

Before getting on the plane, I have to check in at the gate and ask that the wheelchair be tagged so it can be stored under the plane. I am able to transfer from my wheelchair to my crutches and walk onto the plane. I am the first person on the plane. A plus. I am the last one off. Not a plus. When the plane lands, I cross my fingers and hope that my chair gets to me in one piece (it has been dropped and broken on some flights). So, for Ty, this whole process was an exercise in patience—thankfully, he has an ample supply.

I had lived in New York, on Long Island, for eighteen years, but as soon as we landed, everything felt different. I didn't feel like I was coming home. I was scared. The situation had gone from the complete unknown to knowing that something was wrong to now trying to narrow the *something* down—and the scariest part was that no one was taking the "big C" off the table.

What made this trip a bit more stressful was that I had to inform my family that my new boyfriend of six months was traveling with me and staying with me wherever we would end up staying. I was charting new territory by introducing this relationship to my family. I was most anxious about introducing my grandparents to Ty as I had never introduced them to a "boyfriend" before, and their acceptance meant the world to me.

Ty's first meeting with them was at a Shabbos dinner at their summer house on Long Island. We were staying in NYC that first night, so we took a taxi there. During the hour-long ride, I tried to prepare Ty for what the ceremonial dinner would be like while reassuring him that my grandparents would welcome him with open arms. I was right. They opened their home and their hearts to him. They asked Ty all about himself and in return, he asked about them and their background. This thrilled my grandparents, and they were only too happy to share some of their remarkable life stories about growing up in Brooklyn and later on Long Island through sixty-two of marriage. Ty didn't get much time with his grandparents before they passed, so it was fascinating to him to experience their relationship.

We stayed at my mom's house for a couple of days while Ty got acclimated to my unique family dynamic and endured being introduced to family members on each side multiple times. Our relationship at this point was not perfect, but not as strained as it has become. My father had made arrangements through my stepsister's father-in-law to meet with an internist named Dr. Arnie Weg, who they believed would be able to analyze everything and recommend a course of action.

During my first visit with him, I was still very cold, feeling flu-like, and hoping that maybe this was all just a very bad infection. Dr. Weg gave me a complete examination and, after setting aside the potential flu diagnosis, recommended that I get a Positron Emission Tomography (PET) scan. So, off we went to another doctor's office to get that done.

PET scans use radioactively labeled tracers (radiotracers) that are injected into the bloodstream and provide an image of the lump (in my case). That is the simple explanation. What that translates to for the patient is more involved. First, a nurse starts an IV to inject the tracer into a vein. Once that is done, you get moved to a quiet, dark room where you have to lie still for maybe an hour while your body absorbs the injected compound, which is mostly glucose. So, when I was having the scan done, my thinking was, *why can't I just eat a shitload of radioactive candy bars?!* That's an insight into my mood at the time.

So, you lie there in silence so that the tracer material doesn't collect on your tongue and vocal cords. When that part is completed, they lie you on a padded table that slides into the large PET scan machine opening with your arms over your head. The machine looks about the same as a CAT scan machine. You have to lie there, perfectly still, for up to an hour or more. The people with you normally stay in the waiting area, pacing the whole time or drinking vending machine coffee. But for Ty, it meant sitting silently with me in that prep room and occasionally holding my hand or having a one-sided conversation. It was what seemed like the longest hour of my life.

The images from the scan are in color, and they show the areas where tissue is normal and where a tumor or lump has absorbed an inordinate amount of the tracer. When the results were presented to Dr. Weg and then to us, he said they were lit up like a Christmas tree with a lot of the wrong color. Ordinarily, that comment might have invoked a different reaction from my Jewish family than from Ty's Christian background, but in this circumstance, we all took it in the same vein: bad news.

Dr. Weg recommended that I have a lymph node removed for examination in order to get more precise results. I was beyond scared at this point, but Dr. Weg was honest, thorough, and compassionate. I trusted him. He sent us to Cornell University Hospital. For those of you who have lost count, this would be doctor/hospital visit number eight.

This procedure was unlike the biopsy I had undergone. This was actual surgery: more invasive than a simple needle. I awoke from surgery with my father on one side of me, my mom on the other side, and Ty at the foot of my bed. As I came to, I could tell I was about to hear news that I didn't want to hear but that some part of me was expecting. The full diagnosis would not be presented to us for another week, but they knew an abridged version. It was just what I wanted to endure: *more waiting.*

As the days went on, so did life. People still walked down the street, cars and trucks still honked their horns, and I was still very much alive. Then, on May 23, 2016, my life dramatically changed, and not for the better. That was the day I was given the paperwork with my full diagnosis on it: *Stephanie Mikala Hammerman, 26, Hodgkin's Lymphoma Stage 3B.* After two weeks in NYC and after many medical tests, conversations with doctors, and one full lymph-node biopsy, I finally had my answer: it was confirmed that cancer had found my address, knocked on my door, and forced its way inside... me. I was the healthiest I had ever been, young, and had so much life to live—and now a new reality, I had cancer.

This was a harsh reality that no one, especially in their mid-twenties, wants to go through. But I wasn't just any mid-twenties patient. I had entered that hospital as an athlete, and now more than ever, I was determined to leave as one and face this disease as one. As I got out of the hospital bed and back into my wheelchair, I knew I was about to be in for the workout of my life. But if my fitness journey taught me anything, it's how to prepare for the unknown and the unknowable.

Ty did everything he could to keep my spirits high that night. I'm not sure many people find out they have cancer and then head to an NYC rooftop and watch the sunset with the person they love, but that's exactly what we did. I had so many questions, and I was really scared, but Ty and I made a promise to each other that we would do our best to stay in the moment. Still, I wondered, *How am I going to share this with the world? Are people going to want to continue their journey with me now that the focus had shifted?* These were just a few of the things that kept running through my head.

A few days later, Ty and I entered Memorial Sloan Kettering Cancer Center in NYC for the first time, where I met with my lifesaver, Dr. Pamela Drullinsky. "Dr. D," as she became known to me, was probably the best person I could have imagined pairing up with to fight this battle. An oncologist, she specialized in Hodgkin's lymphoma and presented herself as kind and gentle, but very direct. Her confidence spilled over onto me and lifted me up when I most needed it. I felt safe and looked after within a few minutes of meeting her.

Dr. D made it very clear to me that we were going to be learning from one another because she had never worked with someone living with CP. We were going to need to have open lines of communication as to how I was feeling and how my body was reacting to treatments.

As soon as she mentioned that, I had a crystal-clear realization: *I know how I am going to make this experience valuable! I am going to use this experience to bring more education and awareness to the medical community to make certain doctors are better equipped in the future to handle patients with CP.* I had no idea what I was about to get myself into, but I knew that if my experience could help better the life of at least one other person, it would all be worth it. For the six months I was under Dr. D's care, I documented everything about my life. I made an extensive journal of everything from my trips to the bathroom to my emotional state at every turn of my experience. I left nothing unsaid or assumed. I wanted this journal to be a sort of guidebook to help both patients with CP and the doctors who would treat them as to what to expect and how treatments and support might be adjusted.

Our appointment lasted about thirty minutes. I asked a lot of questions, but I found her answers to three of them to be the most helpful and probably relatable to someone in their mid-twenties in a new relationship and with only a vague understanding of what cancer does to the body.

1. Am I going to lose my hair?
2. Can we still have sex?
3. Is this curable?

The answer to all three questions was "yes." I was going to lose my hair, though maybe not all of it because my hair was so thick, but it was inevitable. We could still enjoy a healthy sex life, but it was made very clear that we needed to be safe. My body was going to be put through temporary menopause to ensure my eggs were safe for the future, but we could not chance anything. Dr. D's exact words were, "No chemo babies." I loved that she was able to make us laugh while still keeping us informed. Lastly, this was highly curable; I just needed to continue to stay positive, stay active, and do my best to trust in the process.

The plan was as follows: six months of chemo broken down into twelve "cocktails," then every two weeks, sit for about four hours and let the medicine do its job, then every four weeks, get an injection of Lupron (reversible menopause), and then after about seven weeks, get another scan to see where everything stood.

It was a lot of information to process, but before I could do that, there were a few more tests they had to perform. I had no idea that walking in to meet this doctor for the first time would immediately start the healing process, but it did. It seemed like everything was happening so fast and, within minutes, I was lying on a table experiencing some of the worst pain I'd felt in my entire life. I am not a mother, so I have no idea what labor feels like, but a bone marrow exam cannot be far off. Having spastic CP and hyper tone throughout my body definitely added a level of difficulty, but it needed to be done to ensure the cancer had not yet spread to my bones. Luckily for me, it had not.

After the painful procedure was completed, Ty and I went back into the exam room to meet with Dr. D one last time before starting the treatment plan. "Is there anything in your body right now besides what we have already found that hurts you?" she asked. I had one wisdom tooth left, which was growing in. It was very painful, but what did that have to do with cancer? I told her about the tooth, and she told me that it needed to come out immediately. We couldn't risk anything causing other infections. Once again, everything started moving at lightning speed and, within thirty minutes, we were in a cab heading to Long Island to see a dentist to get my wisdom tooth removed.

Looking back at the dentist visit now, it seems comical. Our first encounter began with the dentist trying to exchange some pleasantries.

"How are you doing today? Having a good day?" he asked in the same tone I assumed he used with every patient not using a wheelchair. I responded with, "Yup! Just found out I have cancer, but what's really cool is that I'm the first patient my doctor has worked with who is living with CP."

At first, he gave me a peculiar look, and then he laughed and told me that I had a great attitude. My truth was that sarcasm and laughter were the only way I knew how to handle everything. If I started going down a bad path or gave in to a bad mindset, it would not be good for anyone. So, there I was, twenty-six years old, the fittest I'd been in my entire life, just diagnosed with cancer, and now minus a little wisdom. This was my new normal. This is what life was handing me. I had two choices: I could throw my hands up and let life happen, or I could take control of the situation and live this new normal the only way I knew how—with drive.

ONE DOOR CLOSES, ANOTHER ONE OPENS

Ty got a couple of part-time jobs to help pay for our time in New York, but as the chemo went on, he spent more of his time just keeping me in good spirits and supporting me emotionally. He had already emptied his bank accounts to pay for the trip and had packed up his life in Florida to adjust to mine. When I asked him about this, his simple response was, "I didn't pick up my life; I just went with it." This was the most romantic thing anyone had ever said to me. It was in this moment that I knew he was the man I was going to spend my life with.

I had my good days, I had my really tough days but, all-in-all, I feel extremely lucky to have had the experience I did. Going through chemo is not for the faint of heart. Watching my hair fall out in clumps, my body drastically change without warning and constantly feeling like I still needed to be pleasing the complicated family dynamic; it was truly a miracle that Ty and I made it out stronger than when we arrived.

After living in New York for almost eight months, as I was approaching the finish line of the chemo treatment, Ty and I had a conversation about where we wanted to go next. We knew that our relationship was developing into something deeper, so we started talking about our future. We had met in Florida, where Ty still had family, but we both knew we wanted to try to make a life somewhere new. The hustle and bustle of New York was just a little too much for us to handle, so we easily ruled out that possibility. We looked toward places that made sense financially and met my accessibility needs that were still not too far from both of our families.

On November 18, 2016, we got the good news. My scan had come back completely clean! I was cancer-free, and I was free to go and live my life.

I knew I could never stop coaching, so during my final rounds of chemo, I completed a few interviews over FaceTime and found a gym in North Carolina that was looking for a coach. They had agreed to hire me once I let them know I was settled, and I could start integrating myself into their community. I can't remember exactly how we stumbled on the idea of possibly moving to North Carolina other than knowing that it was halfway between New York and Florida, but once we did, we were excited to be embarking on a brand-new experience and creating a whole new adventure.

It took about six weeks to get everything settled to move to North Carolina, but as soon as we got that green light, we were excited to start this next chapter of our lives. My doctors were very supportive of our move and made certain that it was a seamless transition to a new set of doctors in a new state. I was cancer-free, but I would still have to be under the care of an oncologist for at least the next five years. It was going to be a long journey, but nothing that I couldn't handle. I'm extremely grateful that I had as much support as I did, especially from Dr. Drullinsky. I will forever be grateful that she not only listened to me but wanted to learn from me (and I from her). She made it clear that this experience was going to come with some emotional baggage from time to time, but she made me promise her that I would live my life to the fullest and never let it define me.

Looking back on it now, selecting North Carolina for our new home was a bit of a crapshoot. But Ty has a saying that I have grown to love: *Real adventures don't start until all your plans have gone to shit.* We had no idea at the time that this place was going to be the foundation for great success in our future.

We only knew one couple in the state, who I had met through social media. The husband had CP and the wife did not, so there was connection there. They gave us their perspective on what it was like to live as an inter-abled couple, including having to deal with seasonal changes and getting around. We tried to ask as many questions as possible, from questions about accessibility to social experiences to the cost of living. A few weeks before our move, Ty went to North Carolina and found us a nice little apartment in the town of Knightdale that he spent about two weeks making accessible for me. We had never heard of this town before; all we knew was that it was about twenty minutes east of Raleigh and close to the gym where I would be working.

Part of me was nervous, and the other part was excited. I hadn't been coaching since April, and I wondered if

I would still be considered a good coach and if I still knew what I was doing. I hoped that coaching was like riding a bicycle and not something that could be completely forgotten in just a few short months, but it was important to me that I continued to sharpen my skills. I reached out to CrossFit headquarters to see if they had an upcoming Level 2 course in or around the tri-county area of North Carolina. I wanted to continue my education and to make certain that my coaching would be on solid ground when I started at the new gym; the L-2 (level two) course would help me do that. Fortunately, things started to align. CrossFit HQ graciously agreed to let me attend the L-2 seminar for free. I now had classes to attend, a new job lined up, and a place to live. And, I had my true love with me, ready to start this new adventure together.

The move happened on Thanksgiving Day in 2016. As we drove to the airport that day, I felt as though a weight had been lifted from my shoulders. For the first time in a long time, I could take a deep breath and know that I was healthy, safe, and in a relationship with somebody who would stick by me regardless of the challenges that we might face. I'd be lying if I said it wasn't nerve-racking moving to a state where you knew almost no one, but at the same time, it was thrilling to know that we had the ability to write our own story. I had been given a second chance at life…again…and I was going to do my best to make the most of it.

Once we were allowed to start moving our things into our apartment, Ty decided to fly back to Florida to pick up my car and drive it back to North Carolina. It was a big trip, but it was an amazing feeling knowing that someone cared for me enough to put such an effort into making sure that I could be as independent as possible. While Ty was on his road trip, I worked with a few new acquaintances I had met at the gym who volunteered to help get our new apartment all set up. I am the type of person who wants to feel settled immediately, so I tried to jam-pack as much as I could into just a few days to turn this apartment into our new home. Little by little, with the hanging of each picture frame and the placing of each piece of artwork, and a few new pieces of furniture I acquired, I made this new apartment feel like ours.

I was so pumped to be starting at the new gym, and I was excited to drive again and to renew my sense of normalcy. It's funny how your brain plays tricks on you. After not doing something for a long time, you wonder if you might have lost the skill altogether. When Ty pulled into the parking lot with my car after his three-day road trip, I was a little bit nervous to get behind the wheel. Being able to drive is a luxury and a skill that I do not take for granted, and I wondered if I would forget how. Sitting in that driver's seat again reminded me of why driving was so important to me. The first time I was allowed to try driving was when I was nineteen. After calling a few different vocational rehab centers in Florida, I was matched with a driving instructor named Ray who was willing to teach me how to drive a car with hand controls. Ray was in his late sixties with a calming demeanor, and he reminded me of my grandpa. That took a lot of the stress out of the equation. I told him how doubtful so many people were about me driving when I was in high school. He looked at me and said, "Well, you won't know if you can drive unless you get in the car." He was right.

My first driving lesson was in Ray's little Honda that was adapted so the instructor could take control of the car from the passenger side. That is pretty standard for instructor cars, but as a driver from the adaptive community, there are more specific changes that have to be made. For one thing, instead of foot pedals, I had a push-pull hand-control device that was connected to both the brake and the accelerator. To accelerate, you pull the bar toward you, and to brake, you push it away from you. And, on the steering wheel is a helpful device commonly referred to in the adaptive community as the suicide knob. Without it, doing wide turns with the hand-over-hand technique would be impossible because one hand has to be on the push-pull device at all times.

I had attended driver ed classes in high school and had already passed the written exam, so I knew the basic rules of the road. Once Ray gave me instructions on how the push-pull and suicide knob worked, we were ready to go. I buckled my seatbelt, checked my mirrors, clicked on the turn signal, engaged the brake, put it in drive, and off we went. I was so nervous, that it took five to ten minutes before I realized I was driving. At first, we drove on the streets I was familiar with. After I aced that part, Ray insisted I take on driving on the highway. So off we went onto Interstate 95. Merging into highway traffic was an eye-opening experience, but once we got safely into a lane, I had a moment of euphoria as we sped down that highway at sixty-five miles per hour. Sixteen driving lessons with Ray later, I passed the driving portion of the test and received my driver's license. To celebrate, my grandparents bought me a car, completely customized to my needs. As they would often be in my life, they were there to make certain I had everything I needed. But the gift they had given me was more than the keys to an expensive custom car. That was incredible. The greater gift was the keys they had given me to a life of full independence.

Driving gave me a sense of independence and confidence that I am grateful to have. So, when I got back behind the wheel after eight months of not driving, I couldn't help but feel a bit emotional and excited to be able to have that independence back.

Luckily for me, I hadn't forgotten how to drive. I now had the means to be able to go anywhere that I needed or wanted to go without having to rely on anyone else or once again feel as though I was burdening someone. I could finally drive myself to the gym, introduce myself to the owner as someone independent, and hopefully accept a job that I knew would be fulfilling.

For my first meeting with the gym owner, I asked Ty to come with me. Not only did I want his opinion, but we also wanted to start exploring the area together, so this was a great excuse. As we pulled into the parking lot of 12th State CrossFit, I began to get a little nervous. *What if they don't take me seriously?* Before my mind could firmly instill that doubt, I took a deep breath and remembered why I was there: Fitness is what I was passionate about, what I was good at, and what I could bring to their community. I shook off the doubts and entered the facility with renewed confidence.

This particular CrossFit was pretty impressive. It was very clean, well-organized, and the people inside were laughing, supporting each other, and seemingly having a great time. We had walked in just when a class was ending. As the people exited the building, Cliff, the owner, came over, smiled, shook my hand, and welcomed us in.

Cliff and I talked for about thirty minutes before he reiterated his commitment to bringing me on staff. I would have to complete a three-week "internship"—shadow a few classes and get to know his community—but once that was done, I would be an official part of the 12th State CrossFit coaching staff. After we agreed to all of this and I left, I was beaming with excitement and pride. The three-week internship experience would give me the opportunity and time to dust off my coach's hat, sharpen my skills, and introduce my unique perspective to a whole new community.

In the beginning, I enjoyed getting to know the community: the athletes were friendly, the other coaches were open-minded, and I began to rekindle the love for what I was doing. Coaching gives you the ability to change people's lives for the better and being able to get to do that every day was a blessing. Unfortunately, my time with this community was going to be cut short.

As my three-week internship was coming to a close, Cliff asked me to meet with him to talk about a few things. Earlier that morning, he had given me many compliments about my coaching style. I figured this meeting was only going to involve the formality of hiring me just before the new year. To my surprise, the meeting was to tell me that I was not going to be on the staff after all. They had decided to hire another coach full-time and because of that, there would be no room for me on the coaching staff. I was shocked and speechless except to ask why. I got some mumbled, unsatisfying response to my question and just wheeled my way out of the gym. Cliff followed me out and, as we went, he offered me the opportunity to continue coaching as an unpaid intern— and if an opening became available, he said, we could talk again about being hired. I thought about it for a moment, but I knew I was worth more than that and didn't want to be somebody's second choice, so I turned him down.

I was truly devastated. I went to my car and just sat there and sobbed. Looking back, I think I was so upset in part because I had feared rejection so much. Now, just when I felt assured that rejection wasn't going to be the outcome, I was proven wrong and was facing the truth I had feared. I knew that I had a lot to offer and that my style of coaching would help me continue to change people's lives for the better. This place wasn't where I was going to do that. I had to live with that reality, but I also had to move on.

During this time, I had been getting weekly massage therapy at another CrossFit location where I had also shifted my workouts. There were several CrossFit locations in the tri-county area, so I had some choices. I formed relationships at the various gyms and then asked if they were in need of a trainer. Fortunately, a couple of the gyms were looking for a trainer part-time, so we remained in North Carolina for about a year while I worked at the different gyms and took stock of my life.

That meant taking a good, hard look at what I truly wanted to do. The communities I had the opportunity to be part of were wonderful, but it was obvious that something was missing—something that I had wanted to create for a very long time.

About four years prior to moving to North Carolina, I had a conversation with my grandfather about opening up a facility where able-bodied people and people in the adaptive community could come together and take part in a fitness experience. I had talked to my grandpa about owning a gym before and then, one night while we were relaxing in our North Carolina home, Ty and I had a similar conversation. He told me that if this was truly something I wanted to do, he would help in any way he could and support me completely.

My grandpa had always been into fitness. He liked to exercise, played a lot of tennis, and was always very active. Even at eighty-four, he still rides horses. He also developed an interest in creating a facility for older adults to engage in fitness and stay active. Both of my grandparents had always been supportive of every move that I made my entire life, and when I broached the subject of having my own gym, they became extremely passionate about it. They insisted on getting involved and helping to make this idea become a reality. With Ty's support and my grandparents' support and financial backing, we began the long process of opening a gym.

I will be the first to admit that this experience was way more challenging than I had ever imagined. From securing a location, building out said location, procuring all of the equipment, and finding the right people to help build this community, it was the toughest thing I'd ever taken on.

We looked at several spots and met with a variety of contractors before settling on what we thought was the perfect location and building. The area was easily accessible and centrally located, which meant we wouldn't have an issue attracting people to the site. But there were some challenges with the building. It was completely gutted— just a shell of a building. It would take a lot to build it out and turn it into a gym. After many days considering the challenges that would go with that build-out, we decided the building was not so perfect after all and abandoned that site. But diagonally across from that building was an empty former bounce-house building. Because we liked the location, we got curious and, during one of our many trips to the site, looked in the windows. The building was a lot of glass and empty space, and it immediately said "fitness" to us. It was larger than we initially wanted, which may be why it was never considered earlier. But we couldn't ignore the message from the universe that this was our perfect building, so we leased it. In actuality, this all took months of going back and forth, but I thought I would spare you that angst and tedium!

***

If it wasn't for Ty, our fitness facility, Hammer Driven Fitness in Knightdale, North Carolina, would never have been possible. Together, we created the cleanest, the most organized, and one of the most aesthetically pleasing places you could ever enter—in my opinion. From installing all of the equipment to rolling out the flooring, to creating the logos and marketing materials, Ty did it all. In one month, he had taken a five-thousand-square-foot shell and turned it into a beautiful gym. While Ty was busy building, I set out to find another trainer to add to our coaching staff. I got lucky as one of the trainers I had befriended from another gym was looking for a change and agreed to take a chance on our new enterprise.

We had the space, we had the equipment, we had a small coaching staff. On September 8, 2018, Hammer Driven Fitness had its grand opening. More than forty people showed up to work out, buy apparel, and show their support. I even sold our first memberships that day. It felt like a successful opening day and one I will never forget.

Through word of mouth, social media marketing, and meeting with other local business owners, we began to create a unique community of members. Normally, if you walk into a CrossFit gym, you will find younger people—people who are serious about preparation for a particular sport or training for competition. But at Hammer Driven Fitness, we embraced people who were different, new to fitness, and not competitive—people just wanting to create a better version of themselves. Another unique thing about our gym is that we never wanted an adaptive athlete or any athlete to feel left out or ostracized for their abilities or lack thereof. Everyone entered our gym as an individual, and they left feeling recognized as an athlete. We were a small but mighty group, and I was proud of what we had built. I liked to describe our small community as lovable misfits. But what they actually were was a group of some of the most wonderful people I could ever have met.

A couple of weeks before the grand opening, Ty and I went to IHOP for breakfast. While we were waiting for our order, I noticed a beautiful woman of about forty who was a wheelchair user. She was sitting with her brother. I decided to approach her uninvited and introduce myself. She told me her name was Nadine and, after a bit of chat, she explained that she had spina bifida from birth. I suggested she would benefit from joining our gym and invited her to our grand opening. She was doubtful as to how she could possibly fit in at a gym but said she would try to make it to the opening. Nadine lived thirty to forty minutes away from the gym and had no independent means of transportation. Still, she surprised me by taking public transit to get to the opening. She didn't work out. She just watched. Afterward, she told me that she studied how I instructed a demonstration class and catered to each athlete's individual needs. She said she was thrilled to find such a welcoming, accommodating place and trainer. So, she signed up for a membership. From then on, Nadine took the bus three times a week without fail for her training. Her dedication to her health and wellness motivated me to always be at my best. She showed true dedication, and I loved her for it.

Around the time I met Nadine, I got an email from a woman named Amanda. She said she was a fan of mine and had been following me for years, from the time I was in Florida until the opening of my gym in North Carolina where she now lived. She jokingly said that she had been stalking me over the years. She was grateful that I had opened a gym in NC that was focused on helping people with adaptive needs as well as seniors. She was really nervous about getting back into CrossFit. She had done it over the years but was forced to stop because of injuries. Now, she wanted to get back into shape. She described herself as "a woman of 50 who has the knees of a ninety-year-old." She had a lot of pain and limited mobility, which she thought would hinder her. She came to the gym, and we assessed her movement and limitations. Then we talked about what we could do together to improve it. I told her she had to be patient and, though I promised her I would never do anything to harm her, I said that I would certainly push and encourage her to find her potential. She was with us from the time we opened until we closed. Over time, she was able to lift more weight, increase her functional strength, and even attempt squats—something her knees would never have allowed her to do before. Her confidence as an athlete and, more importantly, as a person grew over that time as well, and that was a joy to see. She is still a member of the online version of my gym.

Suzanne was unlike any person I had ever met. She was hesitant to start a physical fitness regimen but knew she needed a better quality of life and needed to get her body moving. She had spent many years as a nurse and was unhappy with her appearance. But her main goal was to be healthier for her grandchildren, who she cared for often. She wanted to be able to go up and down the stairs and get up off the floor as she played with the kids and generally just keep up with their energy.

Suzanne was in her sixties when we met. She had a larger-than-life personality. When she entered a room, you definitely knew she was there. She was loud, very foul-mouthed, and you either loved her brassiness or hated it. I enjoyed her directness and full character. She was also one of the kindest, most considerate people you could ever want to know.

Suzanne lost more than twenty-five pounds training with us, and her confidence grew beyond her brassiness as she took on heavier weights without fear. Like Nadine and Amanda, she showed up every day for the nine a.m. ladies class, and they formed a camaraderie and a dedication to one another. If one of them missed a class, the others were certain to call and make certain that all was well. We still stay in touch even though she could not make the transition from in-person to online training. She thrived on the encouragement and face-to-face motivation from me and the others to help bring her through the workouts. I think she also needed and enjoyed the closeness of the nine, a.m. group that she didn't find online.

Clayton is one of my best friends. He was an architecture student at the time we were building the original gym site and working with Tony Johnson Architecture.

The first time I walked into their office, I was confronted with Clayton's bright, welcoming smile and his calm demeanor. I was drawn to him immediately. His evenness helped me get through the angst of trying to design a giant space from bottom to top. We eventually abandoned that potential site and ended our relationship with the architecture firm, but I remained in touch with Clayton.

When we built the new space, I invited him to the opening, but he didn't make it. I then invited him to the gym fairly often, but to my dismay, I couldn't get him to come in. Then, on our first Christmas Eve in the gym, I invited him to a Christmas-themed workout aptly called "The Twelve Days of Christmas." Instead of partridges in pear trees, the athletes performed different exercises that matched the progression of the songs. So, five golden rings might become five deadlift squats and so on. This time, he showed up, and to my surprise, participated in the themed workout. By the end of the routine, he was lying on his back, breathing heavily and exhausted. But he had the biggest smile on his face. Once he was able to peel himself off the ground, we sat down and talked about what he thought about working with us, and he signed up for a membership. I had him.

He continued to embrace his membership and the workouts and eventually became so physically strong that his shyness was replaced with confidence. He is still one of my athletes, still one of my very best friends, and we FaceTime almost every day.

Each day, someone would tell me about the changes they were making for themselves and the positive impact this community was having on their lives. It was those small reminders that kept me going. I loved creating a space where people could feel comfortable to be themselves and be proud of their achievements.

***

In the beginning, before the doors even opened, I had a lot of people tell me that I would be a great gym owner. They said people would be flocking to my gym because everyone loves Steph "The Hammer" Hammerman! Well, the reality was that after opening day, things got extremely difficult. Bringing in paying members was a challenge, and growing the business to be sustainable felt impossible. A few months after opening, I had the opportunity to share my story with the world on *Good Morning America*, and I had to take it.

I don't always know who is following me on social media, and it surprises me at times. One particular follower was a woman named Reni, a producer for Robyn Roberts, a host of *Good Morning America*. She messaged me on Instagram telling me that she was following my story and wanted to speak with me. I emailed her.

> Me: Good morning, Reni! I saw your message on IG last night. Sorry I didn't respond earlier. It was my birthday yesterday and my phone was pretty crazy! Haha. People definitely know how to make a girl feel loved!
>
> How may I help you? I can't believe someone at GMA knows about me! Haha. I'm a religious watcher!

Have a wonderful day!

Steph

Reni: Happy birthday!!!!

I'd love to jump on a call with you to ask you some questions. There's a series we are developing and I think you'd be a great fit.

Are you available today to chat?

Reni

And that's how it got started. I spoke with Reni on the phone, and she told me that GMA was doing a spotlight series on motivation. Reni had been following me for a long time on social media and was a fellow CrossFitter, and she thought my story was a perfect fit with the show. After coordinating the time to do this, the show sent a camera crew to Hammer Driven Fitness. We did the live interview with Robyn Roberts and her studio audience from my gym. It all happened that quickly.

I was a bit nervous. I had been on CNN when I was a kid and again a few years back, but that was a taped interview. This was a live segment for a major national show, and I wasn't as carefree about things as a kid might be. And this was a show that I followed, so I was nervous and really wanted it to go well. And it did. I got exposure to millions of people from all over the world and media attention from everywhere. I received hundreds, maybe even a thousand messages from people wishing me well and encouraging me with positivity. Parents of kids with CP and others living with CP reached out to tell me how inspiring it was to hear my story and see me doing what I do.

I was truly hoping that this interview would bring more people into the gym, but as wonderful as the story might have been, not everybody lived near Knightdale, North Carolina.

> *Sustaining the gym was becoming a constant struggle. I had bitten off more than I could chew when it came to the cost to run the business, keeping people happy, and keeping my sanity. My relationship with Ty was being tested as well, and just when we thought the challenges couldn't get worse, a year and a half into the business, we were having to navigate a global pandemic. It was at this point that I had to have an honest conversation with myself, Ty, and my grandparents. I had failed. I couldn't keep my head above water, and it was obvious that if we stayed open, we would be doing more harm than good. I was devastated. I had told everyone this was my dream, and now I couldn't sustain that dream. Maybe I concentrated too much on making everyone happy and not enough on the business side of things. All that was certain was that this business could not survive, and it hit me hard.*

We were mandated by the state to close our doors to

our athletes for the foreseeable future in order to keep them safe. We had no idea how long that would be, but I couldn't just sit idly by and wait. Once a few days turned into a few weeks, we started hosting our classes for our members online. They were still paying for membership, so we did our best to give them the best experience we could while working out at home. To my surprise, it was working—members were attending the online classes and even staying on afterward to socialize for a bit.

I told my grandma I was hosting these workouts, and she asked me if I would be willing to host a workout for a group of women with disabilities. In 1997, she had created a program called the Initiative for Women with Disabilities hosted out of NYU Hospital. Now, due to the pandemic, all of their in-person programming had been canceled until further notice. Without hesitation, I said yes to my grandma, and we began to run these free classes twice a week for a group of twenty to thirty-five women. Week after week, it became clearer that we had a recipe for success.

As this started to grow, I realized I needed help. My good friend Kelli lived about twenty-five minutes away from me, but she had sent me a message telling me to reach out to her if I ever needed anything. We all have people in our lives who say those words, but Kelli was different. She truly meant it. When I reached out to her and told her what I had been doing with these online classes and the success we were having, she told me without reservation that she wanted to be involved and reiterated that she would do anything I needed to help.

It was clear that the pandemic was here to stay. Weeks turned into months, and we knew we were going to have to make it known to our athletes and the greater community that we would be closing the doors of HDF for good. As the saying goes, though...

When one door closes, another one opens.

As we started building a client base, Ty and I started developing a new business plan. Staying Driven, LLC still had the heart of Hammer Driven but was accessible to people all over the globe. We had no idea how long it was going to last, but what was unfolding in front of our eyes was pretty special to witness.

It was clear that we were saying goodbye to one business and that some loose ends needed to be tied up, but did we have to stay in North Carolina to be successful? We had a few deeper conversations and came to the conclusion that as long as we were together and healthy, we could go anywhere in the world and be successful. We had lived in North Carolina for about three-and-a-half years. In that time, I had continued to conquer cancer, and we learned how to disagree and how to make up. We had learned the difference between friends and acquaintances and also what it meant to be responsible for an animal after bringing home a seven-and-a-half-week-old husky lab that we named Hexi.

As more information about the pandemic became available, the idea of moving became more real. Our time in North Carolina had been great but, besides Hexi, we didn't have anything tying us down. Travel was being completely restricted, and we weren't sure the next time we were going to be able to see my grandparents, so we started having real conversations about what our next move would look like. Similar to what we did when we lived in New York, we made a list of the states we could see ourselves living in. We agreed the most logical option for us would be Arizona.

We decided to keep the online training free for the next ninety days while we created a new schedule of classes, a new logo, and a new website. It wasn't long before I was able to hire Kelli and another coach named Jordy. Jordy's situation was unique because we had never met in person, but after seeing her interact during one of the group classes and finding out about all the knowledge she had as a Doctor of Physical Therapy, I knew I had to hire her on the spot. We started this business with a small amount of capital, and they were both willing to donate their coaching services until we really got up and running. It was a gift. With their help, we were able to offer a few different class times. People joined the classes whenever they were available and shared the Staying Driven story and website with anyone they felt could benefit from the program.

Staying Driven was in its infancy stage, but people began buzzing about us. We had people coming day after day, week after week wanting to continue their workouts.

Kelli and I had become the best of friends. She was someone I could truly count on, and I was so glad we were doing this together. Kelli and I had never met Jordy, but after the first week of working with her, we felt like we had known her for a lifetime. It was amazing to see and feel the great things that people who believe in the same mission can accomplish.

In the first few weeks, we had more than thirty people signing on for the classes daily. It was fascinating to me to realize that you don't need four walls and a white-board to create a successful fitness community and a positive environment. But the question remained, would people keep coming back if they had to start paying for the training? We were, after all, a business, this was my job, and I couldn't continue to work for free.

Ty had the idea that we offer "a lot for a little": give people a quality experience for an affordable price. So, we set out with a plan to sell memberships for $20 a month. If people wanted to join for one month, they could, and if for any reason they needed to cancel, there would be no pressure, no contract, and they could cancel at any time and rejoin at any time.

I was a little nervous because I felt like we might be pricing the experience a little too low, but I knew that all I had to do was trust Ty's plan. We decided that the last week of June would be the best time for us to start on our road trip to the desert. We had been dating for four-and-a-half years; everyone always assumed that we were married. It always made us laugh because people would call us husband and wife, and I often wondered if people assumed that just because of the way we interacted with one another.

Back in New York, while my cancer battle was rag-ing and we were somewhat newly dating, I began to lose my hair. Ty told me that he thought I was so beautiful and that I needed to keep fighting because he wanted to spend the rest of his life loving me. I was a little taken back because I had never heard anybody profess love to me like that. If he could love me at my worst then I was confident he would love me exactly as I am for the rest of our lives. And, I figured he had earned my trust.

We had five days of driving ahead of us. At first, I wanted to keep Hexi with Ty to help keep him awake while driving for so long, but we soon learned that she felt way more comfortable being near me and my wheelchair. I was like her safety blanket. So, we traveled for four days, caravan style.

July 2, the last day of our drive, we were in New Mexico. We were about four hours away from our destination when our caravan came across La Ventana Arch. We had very bad cell phone reception, but for some reason, Ty's call came through. "Babe, look to your left. How beautiful! Do you want to stop and take a few pictures?" Of course I did! Number one, I love pictures, and number two, this place was gorgeous. I was also excited to take a little bit of a break. I had Hexi in the car with me, and I was fully expecting him to tell me to leave her in the car, but to my surprise, he wanted her to come out and take a family photo with us. I was so excited about taking the photo, that I didn't think anything of it.

We walked around for a bit and took in the site. It was breathtaking. Every time I use my wheelchair when we take photos, Ty gets down on one knee to be level next to me. Our running joke up to that point was...one of these days, he'll do that for real. Well, as he got down on one knee and got the phone set up to take a picture, he asked me to take something from his hand and hold onto it for him. I looked down and in the middle of his palm was a beautiful diamond! To which I so kindly responded, "Are you joking? That's not mine!" He wasn't joking, and it was mine! He really wanted *me* to be his wife! I laughed and cried so many happy tears and couldn't stop staring at the ring that Ty had placed on my ring finger on my left hand. He had chosen me. He'd chosen me a long time ago, and I was so ready for this. For a girl who never believed she would ever find true love by swiping right, this was a moment I will forever cherish.

Just when I thought everything was falling apart, I remembered the old saying that good things fall apart so that greater things can come together. This is my journey, and it's only just begun.

STAYING DRIVEN

I'll admit that it's quite strange how easily our new business model came together. After struggling with the feeling of intense shame and failure of the physical space closing, it was hard to accept that this really was working and wasn't too good to be true.

It's now just about two years into the new business, as well as the business of being a married woman, and I can say with confidence that both are doing well. I am proud to say that we have not only maintained our original business model but that we have improved it in ways that I don't think any of us could have pictured while sitting in Hammer Driven Fitness trying to figure out our next steps.

Kelli and Jordy stayed true to their word, and so did we. As soon as we had paying members, we were proud to put them on the payroll and pay them for their time, commitment, and dedication to our community. In the time that we have been in business, we have grown to a staff of eight coaches, including those within the adaptive community, from across the country and Canada. Collectively, the business offers thirty live virtual classes a week, each led by a certified instructor. We offer individual memberships as well as corporate memberships to a variety of organizations that focus on improving the lives of those who live with different abilities.

Each day, we have the opportunity to enhance the way people perceive what it means to be athletic. You don't need four walls, some heavy weights, and a whiteboard to run a successful fitness business and build a community full of compassionate people.

We are proof that the real adventure doesn't start until all your plans go to shit. This new business model definitely came with a learning curve, but it was a much-welcomed change to the overwhelming nature of owning and operating a five-thousand-square-foot brick-and-mortar business.

The pandemic changed the world as we once knew it forever, and it has taken a lot from a lot of people, forcing them to face some harsh realities and broken dreams. It also created opportunities that never existed before. I might have felt like a failure, but defeat is not even trying to get back up. Staying Driven was my next move, the new way I remind myself that failure is not an option.

IF I CAN DO IT, SO CAN YOU!

When I first started working out, I would train three times a week, and it felt like a lot. As time went on and my abilities increased as well as my knowledge, so did my workouts. By the time I was five years into training and the competitive adaptive movement, I began working out two to three times a day. I liked to think of it as a healthy obsession. Now in the community for ten years, and five years after my cancer diagnosis, my training has definitely changed, and so have my priorities.

My body went through some drastic changes while undergoing chemo. In some ways, I felt as though I no longer had a recognizable physical version of myself that I had been seeing in the mirror for so many years. I had gained a ton of weight, my body often felt weak, and it was hard to see me. It's been five years since that drastic change occurred, and while I am way more active and have lost a lot of the weight, it's still not easy to remember the person that I once was so proud of.

I still love fitness, and I'm extremely passionate about the community, but I don't work out because I'm a competitive athlete. I work out to live a functional and happy life. Today, I am more focused on my overall well-being, health, and functionality. My competitive spirit will always be part of me, but now I am more focused than ever on keeping other people functional and in motivating others to make their health and well-being a priority. I have come to enjoy coaching other people more than being in the competitive spotlight. Coaching gives me the opportunity to constantly sharpen my skills while motivating others to believe in themselves more than they ever would by working out alone.

I once heard that if you find a path without any obstacles, it probably doesn't lead anywhere worth your time. As I've gotten older and have had the opportunity to share my life with so many, it's been important to me to recognize that I was born with CP for a reason.

I use tools like fitness challenges and a smartwatch to keep me motivated, and I surround myself with people who want to see me succeed and help hold me accountable. Our time on this planet is valuable. I truly believe I was put on a different path than most because I have a greater purpose. My life, my will, my drive are meant to be on display so that the next little one born with CP knows they have the ability to live out their dreams and change the world.

Inspiration (noun):
> *The process of being mentally stimulated to do or feel something, especially to do something creative.*

I hear the word "inspiration" just about every single day of my life. So much so that to me, the word feels empty. I've become jaded. Why?

People say things like, "You're such an inspiration. Just seeing you out and about helps me get out of bed when I'm having a bad day." Or, "It's so inspiring to see you do what you do. If I were you, I could never do it." Such statements make me realize that the definition of the word "inspire" includes feeling something and that these good people are sharing a feeling, but there is no commitment in that feeling. There is no related action that would show me just how I inspired them to improve their lives. Add to that that these comments, though not meant to be hurtful, can be condescending: *Poor little wheelchair girl, how do you have a life? You actually got up in the morning and got dressed and made it to the mailbox.*

Not so long ago, I had a conversation with a woman I did not know but who I could tell was trying to come from the best place possible while speaking to me. But by the end of the conversation, I felt frustrated. She had taken what she perceived to be my "struggles" and used them as her inspiration to get out of bed and have a productive day. Here's how this encounter went.

It was late afternoon around five p.m., and I decided to go for a bike ride. I like riding around that time of day because it's not too hot, the sun is close to setting, and the views in my neighborhood are spectacular. We live on a really quiet cul-de-sac, and the neighbors are pretty friendly. I ride my bike or do some sort of physical activity outside almost every day, so I don't ever really think about who could be watching me. In this particular instance, however, I was in the middle of my ride when I sensed a car slowly approaching from behind me. I moved to the side of the road so they could safely pass me. But, instead of passing, they lurked beside me and as I turned toward the car to see if I was in the way somehow. The female driver stopped the car, rolled down her window, and said, "I just wanted to tell you I think you are so inspiring. I saw you out here with your husband walking, and I just think it's truly unbelievable to see you out here." I smiled, said thank you, and thought she'd be on her way, but she wasn't done. "Sometimes, I don't want to get out of bed, and when that happens, I think about you working so hard out here. It reminds me that I have no excuse," she said.

I'm sorry, but while I know this woman was most likely coming from the best place possible in her heart, what I heard was: *"When I don't want to get out of bed, I think about how hard life must be for you, and it makes me realize I have no excuse."*

Here's why this bothers me. This woman, and a lot of other people for that matter, perceive that *everything* in my life must be a struggle because I have CP. But, I'm just living my life. I work hard because the journey toward achieving my goals is rewarding as hell. I push myself physically every day because I can and because I want to be the best version of myself. My CP requires adjustments other folks may not have to make, but they are part of my way of life and my daily routine. They are much the same, in that respect, as anyone else's. I don't celebrate them.

"It's so nice to see you out here." "It's awesome to see

you get out." These statements drive me nuts. My house is not a cage. I don't have a handler who grants me freedom. I am not "out." I am living my best freaking life! Some people need to tell me so badly that my physical existence and hard work are inspiring, but that leaves me feeling empty because there is no reason for it. I didn't spark a sense of creativity in them; I make them feel ashamed instead of empowered.

Motivation (noun):
The reason or reasons one has for acting or behaving in a particular way.

When I was on *Good Morning America* in April 2019 and had the opportunity to sit (remotely) across from host Robyn Roberts, I knew it was my opportunity to share my feelings about the word "inspiring." She asked me a question about the term, and I said this: "I like to think of inspiration as the spark to the motivation that lights a great big fire." I was pretty proud of that answer. When people tell me I inspire them, I often respond with a thank you, but deep down, I wonder what I inspired them to do or change about their life.

This is why I find the words "motivate," "motivation," and "motivational" so much more impactful and empowering. I truly get a thrill out of knowing that I was able to help create a positive change in the lives of others—that I *motivated* them to make that change.

That's a large part of why I wanted to write this book. If there's one thing you take away from this whole story, I hope it's that you understand that there's a huge difference between being inspired and being motivated.

If my hard work inspires you to want to work just as hard as I do, do it. If you are inspired to make daily changes for the better, you must use that inspiration to find motivation. Once you have turned the inspiration into the motivation to make a change, the last ingredient you will need to finish this recipe for success is discipline. Inspiration sparks the motivation, motivation lights the fire, and discipline encourages your actions. If my life story, my motivation, and my actions inspire change within one person, I will know that living out this different blueprint of life is one-hundred percent worth it.

If I could leave you with one piece of advice, it's this: Chase the "yes." Ask the tough questions, carve out opportunities, and when the answer is "no," move on to the next potential opportunity. *Someone* is bound to say "yes," and when they do, use all the "no's" from the past as the fuel for your fire. We all have the power to change the world. You must remain DRIVEN.

CREDITS

This book is a work of art produced by Incorgnito Publishing Press

Robert Cooper
Editor

Star Foos
Cover Designer

Janice Bini
Chief Reader

Daria Lacy
Graphic Production

Michael Conant
Publisher

August 2022
Incorgnto Publishing Press